THE ROYAL MEWS

Also by Mary Stewart-Wilson and David Cripps

QUEEN MARY'S DOLLS' HOUSE

THE ROYAL MEWS

Mary Stewart-Wilson

Photographs by David Cripps

THE BODLEY HEAD
LONDON

DEDICATION
To the past, present and future staff of the Royal Mews.

Title page: Before the State Opening of Parliament the Imperial State Crown is brought from the Tower of London to Buckingham Palace. Here it is placed in Queen Alexandra's State Coach and, ahead of The Queen, is conveyed under escort to the Palace of Westminster.

A CIP catalogue record for this
book is available from the British Library

0 370 313453

© Text Mary Stewart-Wilson 1991
David Cripps's photographs of the
Royal Mews were taken and are here
reproduced by gracious permission
of Her Majesty The Queen
David Cripps's photographs © Her Majesty Queen Elizabeth II 1991
Design by Trevor Wayman
Printed and bound in The Netherlands for
The Bodley Head Ltd
20 Vauxhall Bridge Road, London SW1V 2SA
by Koninklijke Smeets Offset b.v., Weert, Netherlands

First published 1991

Contents

Acknowledgements

This book could not have been written without Her Majesty's consent, for which I am deeply indebted. I would like to thank Her Majesty for her gracious permission to make use of materials from the Royal Archives and the Royal Mews Archives and for her kindness in allowing us so much time to take a completely new set of photographs in the Mews. A proportion of the proceeds of this book will go towards the upkeep of the Royal Collection.

In the Royal Mews I am especially grateful to: the Crown Equerry, Lieutenant Colonel Seymour Gilbart-Denham, and the Superintendent, Major Albert Smith. Also the Comptroller of Stores, Major Leslie Marsham.

In the Royal Mews Office I would like to thank: Chief Clerk Paul Almond, Deputy Chief Clerk Allen Marshall and Office Keeper the late Peter Goodman. My thanks also go to Head Chauffeur David Griffin.

It would have been extremely difficult to write this book without the full co-operation of:

| Head Coachman | Deputy Head Coachman | Coachman | Coachman | Coachman/Rough Rider |
| Arthur Showell | Alfred Oates | Richard Boland | John Nelson | Stephen Matthews |

all of whom have my warmest thanks.

I am also grateful to:

| Serjeant Farrier | Royal Mews Storeman | Senior Livery Helper | State Harness Cleaner | Ascot Room Harness Cleaner |
| Albert Wright | Richard Borer | Joseph Day | Lawrence Oates | Hugh Murphy |

and for the cheerful acceptance of the book team by every member of the Mews staff.

The unstinting help and enthusiasm of Head Carriage Restorer Erik West and his assistant Martin Oates were probably the main reasons that the book team retained their sanity and sense of humour throughout the project and for this they will always have my heartfelt thanks.

For their time and knowledge I would like to thank the following: Captain the Hon Nicholas Beaumont; Lady de Bellaigue; Mr Marcus Bishop; Mr Angus Cundey of Henry Poole & Co. Ltd.; Mr W. G. Whelan and Mr K. Fryer of A. E. Chapman Ltd.; Mr G. C. Francis; Mr Robert Gieves of Gieves & Hawkes; Georgina Gilbart-Denham; Mr W. H. Summers and Mr D. V. Thomas of Garrard & Co. Ltd.; Mr T. C. Highfield of Joseph Mason Plc; Major Edwin Hunt; Mr Christopher Lloyd; Keith Luxford; Mr John Marriott; Mr John McVitty; Lieutenant Colonel Sir John Miller; Mr David Money-Coutts; Mrs Elsie Oates; Lieutenant Colonel Sir Eric Penn; Mr Michael Shillabear; The Lord Somerleyton; Mr Michael Tims; Major John Holman; Mrs W. Weddle; Lieutenant Colonel George West; Mrs Patricia West; Miss Marie Wood, and Rosanna Bickerton.

Finally, my special thanks go to photographic assistant Piran Murphy, designer Trevor Wayman and Jill Black of the Bodley Head for their invaluable contributions towards this book.

I am also indebted to the following for permission to reproduce copyright photographic material: H.M. The Queen, pages 36–7 and 160; The Camera Press, pages 142 and 161; The Hulton Picture Company, page 170; E. J. Collings, pages 14 and 132; Magnum Photos, pages 54–5; Glenn Harvey, page 154; Lionel Cherruault, page 162; John Shelley, page 175; and Tim Graham, page 182 (left).

M. S-W

Foreword by His Royal Highness The Prince of Wales

KENSINGTON PALACE

A stone's throw from one of London's bustling commercial districts, just up the road from one of the city's busiest railway termini, lies a tiny village. The Royal Mews is a village in the fullest sense; a close community of people both live and work there; and it has its own economy, founded upon traditional skills which are still practised there as they have been for centuries.

Stepping through the Mews' gates (and under the clock tower commissioned by the fifth Duke of Dorset - a gesture I wholeheartedly applaud!), it is possible to imagine how a large part of London used to be when it was served by quarters devoted to specialised crafts; when it was full of craftsmen such as watchmakers and jewellers working side by side. If the Mews seems now more like a Museum than a living piece of city it is because most other such quarters have been and are being swept away.

But of course the Royal Mews is far from being a Museum, as this book makes clear. It still serves very practical needs, and is renowned throughout the world for the way in which the horses and carriages are turned out for various Royal and State occasions. As a child I remember only too well the fascination of visits to the Mews and, in particular, when I was taken at the age of four to see the Coronation Coach being prepared for The Queen's Coronation in 1953. I suspect that those childhood visits have given me a lifelong pleasure of travelling in horse-drawn carriages. In that sense I am indebted to my ancestor, King George III, for having established something which continues to give continual enjoyment and interest to countless people all around the world.

Mary Stewart-Wilson has clearly succeeded in vividly conveying the continuing life of the Mews, and showing us how it carries on doing its job with that efficiency and humour which only a great deal of dedication and practice can achieve.

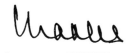

Bibliography

The English Carriage, Hugh McCausland, Batchworth Press, 1948

Men, Women and Things, The Duke of Portland, Faber & Faber Ltd., 1937

Coaching Days of England, Anthony Burgess, Paul Elek Ltd., 1966

Queste, 1988 Automobile Quarterly

Master of the Horse, M. M. Reese, Threshold Books Ltd., 1976

Royal Cavalcade, Marylian Watney, J. A. Allen Ltd., 1987

The Encyclopaedia of Carriage Driving, Sallie Walrond, J. A. Allen Ltd., 1988

Clementine Churchill, Mary Soames, Cassell Ltd., 1979

The Royal Mews, Pitkin Pictorials, 1979

The Australia State Coach, Cynthia A. Foley, Jim Frecklington, Dubbo, 2830, 1988

Royal Heraldry, J. P. Brooke-Little, Pilgrim Press Ltd., 1987

The Coachmakers, Harold Nockolds, J. A. Allen Ltd., 1977

MANUSCRIPT SOURCES

Papers of the Master of the Horse, Royal Archives and Royal Mews

Introduction

Throughout the year British and foreign visitors of all ages stand, sit and queue in all weathers to catch a glimpse of the British Royal Family. Whether viewed on the streets, the television screen or the printed page, many such occasions begin and end with a glimpse of a royal motorcade or, better, a sumptuous horse-drawn procession.

Planned or unintentional, these glimpses leave behind a curiosity in the spectator's mind which can in part be satisfied by a visit to the Royal Mews, because Her Majesty The Queen allows them to be opened to the general public on certain afternoons during the week. Thousands of visitors there enjoy at first hand the atmosphere of a full-time working mews. Centred around the historic buildings and essential work shops, they can see the horses, carriages and state harness that are daily maintained for Her Majesty's use.

The Royal Mews Buckingham Palace is one of the six departments of the Royal Household, whose working members handle the day-to-day business of the Sovereign. Under the Crown Equerry, the department is responsible for providing and co-ordinating the motor and horse-drawn travelling arrangements for The Queen and other members of the Royal Family.

History has shown that royal patronage can play an important part in the pursuit of excellence, and this is reflected in the unique standard of craftsmanship and traditional turnout found in the Mews. These provide an inspiration for the many coaching clubs, carriage associations and driving societies that exist throughout the world today.

Her Majesty's continued use of horse-drawn carriages on both state and domestic occasions is one of the factors that ensures Great Britain remains unequalled in the modern world in terms of ceremonial pageantry. What we have set out to do in this book is visually to stop the procession and allow the bystander a leisurely look at two and a half centuries of tradition and service to the Crown.

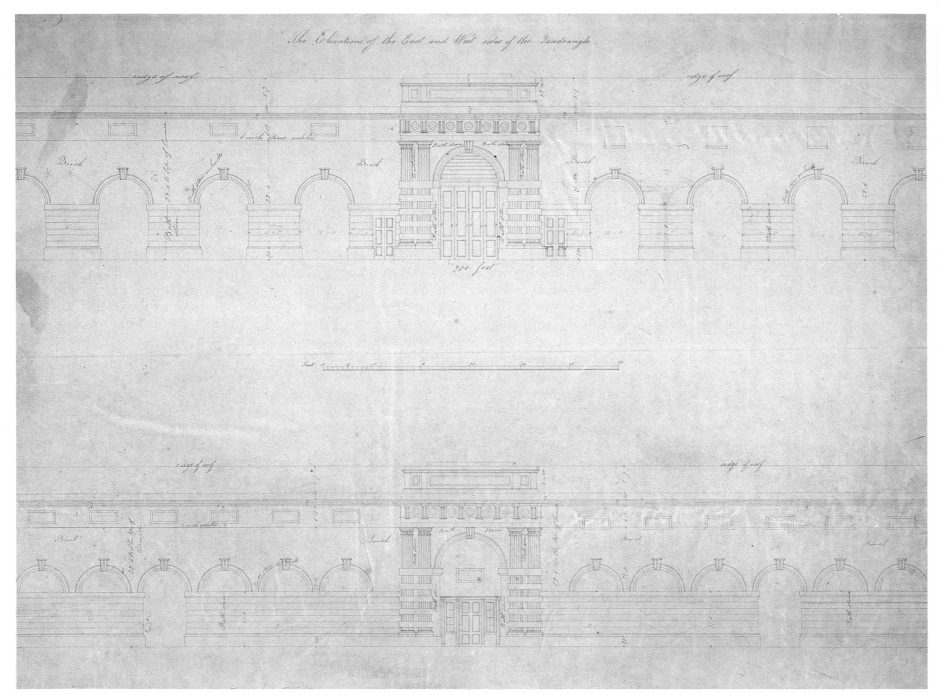

Nash's original plan for the quadrangle.

1 The Story of the Royal Mews

MEW: Old French: *mue*, from *muer*
Latin: *mutare*, to change
To moult, or shed the feathers

New English Dictionary

Behind the large squares and crescents that were built in the eighteenth and nineteenth centuries in major British towns and cities, narrow cobbled streets can still be found today lined with attractive low buildings. These 'mews' were originally areas set aside for the outside staff, horses, carriages, and later the motor cars, of the big city houses. More recently they provided living accommodation above private garages, repair shops, livery stables and riding schools, until in the housing boom of the Fifties and Sixties most of them were converted into flats or elegant houses.

The word 'mews' itself has had an interesting history, much of it linked with the British monarchy, and it was not until the eighteenth century that it was first used in its modern sense. In Saxon England, when the art of falconry was an essential part of a noble upbringing, hawks and falcons were kept near the kennels and stables of a large household. The birds' regular change of plumage was referred to as 'mewing' and during this time, the brooding birds were confined or 'mewed up' in cages. The area they occupied, combined with the stabling and accommodation of the attendant falconers, became known as a 'mews'.

In the thirteenth century a royal mews for falcons was built at Charing Cross in London, where the National Gallery now stands. This became a royal pleasure ground, close to the Palace of Westminster, and it was here three centuries later that Henry VIII (1509–47) mewed his falcons. However, in 1537 fire destroyed his stables in the part of London now known as Bloomsbury. As a result, the King decided to enlarge the mews area at Charing Cross and, moving the birds elsewhere, he established his horses and stable staff there instead.

By 1732 these buildings were so dilapidated that George II (1727–60) asked the architect William Kent to restore the site and design a larger establishment for his stud in the classical style. Only twenty-eight years later, however, the combination of urban building round about and the rapid growth in the use of carriages rendered Kent's stables too small to accommodate all the horses and carriages of the new king, George III (1760–1820). The young king decided to move some of his stud and carriages into the existing stables behind Buckingham House, originally the home of the Duke of Buckingham, which he had just purchased. With the addition of a 'riding house', or indoor school, believed to have been designed by Sir William Chambers in 1765, these stables were referred to as the Royal Mews Pimlico.

After nine years of extravagance as Prince Regent, King George IV (1820–30) was refused funds by the government for the palace that he had planned to build on the site of Buckingham House on his accession in 1820. The government did, however, grudgingly approve a sum of money for the remodelling of the existing house and the rebuilding of the Royal Mews. The King, who wanted a palace that he felt would be worthy of himself and the nation, persuaded a reluctant government to give the commission to his favourite architect, John Nash.

Nash's reputation did not stand very high at the time. Harassed and elderly, he was not particularly anxious to take on the massive and complicated renovations envisaged by the King. Errors made in his initial specifications for the project were added to endless delays which outlasted the King's reign and ensured that George IV never lived in his new palace.

The rebuilding of the Royal Mews was only achieved after three years of constant problems. After accepting the lowest of the seven estimates submitted, the government authorised a sum of £48,565 for work to start in July 1822. The plans were relatively simple. Leaving the existing riding house where it was, Nash designed a Doric arch leading to a large quadrangle. Around this the main coachhouses were laid out on the east side, with blocks of stables divided by forage and harness rooms on the west. Behind a matching Doric arch at the north end of the quadrangle was a back or 'upper' mews, on the west side of which were the official houses for the Veterinary Surgeon and the Equerry of the Crown Stables. Cramped living quarters were found for the Mews staff above the stables and coachhouses, while in front of the main archway at the entrance Nash built a porter's lodge and a handsome house for the Clerk of the Stables and his assistant.

Although in drawing up his plans Nash said he had 'most amply consulted' the Clerk of the Stables, there was a series of structural complications and delays caused by the inadequate briefing he had been given by the officers of the Mews, who then discovered serious flaws in the foundations once the actual building began. The government was constantly forced to pay out further instalments against the rising costs, while the Office of Works and other government departments interfered and delayed progress by arguing between themselves. Nash, meanwhile, severely criticised for his poor planning and inaccurate estimates, left the supervision of the construction to subordinates. They permitted the use of unsatisfactory materials, and the initially high standard of workmanship deteriorated.

Eight months before the 'horses and stables' of His Majesty were installed in their new buildings, the final cost of the Mews project had reached over £65,000. A last-minute addition was the clock tower with the finishing date, 1825, cut into the weathercock. This was ordered at the special request of the Master of the Horse, the fifth Duke of Dorset.

The Keeper of the Royal Stables or Master of the Horse was a power-ful member of the court, with great personal influence on the monarch. He was ranked third great officer of the Royal Household below the Lord Chamberlain and the Lord Steward, a precedence held to this day. Traditionally he was responsible for the provision and organisation of the royal horses, studs and travelling arrangements, and the position was the monarch's personal appointment.

The political importance which originally attached to the posts of all three great officers declined during the eighteenth century, and the appointment of Master of the Horse was rarely affected by political considerations. However, following the fifth Duke of Dorset's resignation as Master of the Horse in 1827 for purely political reasons, the appointment became a government one, and for the next hundred years Masters of the Horse changed with each successive ministry in power.

Although Nash's initial design for the Mews is still instantly recognisable today, once in use the area required constant general repairs and alterations. The inadequate foundations were responsible for sagging balconies, sunken walls and rotten flooring, whilst faulty planning meant a shortage of harness rooms and staff facilities. The Earl of Albemarle, Master of the Horse to George IV's brother, King William IV (1830–37), found it difficult to persuade the government that the Pimlico buildings should be improved. The damp, badly drained coachhouses and stables with their clinkered floors encouraged night-time infestations of black beetles, which put the horses off their feed and ruined the carriages' upholstery, whilst the poorly appointed harness rooms subjected the great quantity of valuable state harness to what he described as 'considerable injury' and consequent 'expense and repair'.

By the end of the reign of William IV the newly invented gas lighting had replaced the old oil lamps and the stable floors had been flagstoned.

Their Majesties King George V and Queen Mary inspecting the royal stables with Princess Mary, 30 May 1912.

It was considered too expensive to flag the coachhouses, but a disused servants' hall was converted into a proper harness room and a stable was curtained and furnished as a staff recreation room. Little else was done to improve the appalling hygiene and overcrowding of the staff quarters. It was many years before the general care and welfare of the Mews families were given priority over the upkeep of horses, harness and carriages.

Queen Victoria came to the throne in 1837, and was the first monarch to use Buckingham Palace as both an official residence and a home. For the first time the Mews and its community, reached by a private drive through the gardens, became an integral part of the 'Big House'.

After their marriage in 1840 Prince Albert took over the use of the back or 'upper' mews for his own stable of riding and driving horses. A new forge was installed and, at the request of the expanding royal nurseries, sheds were erected at the rear of the back mews to house a cow when the family was in residence. This area is still referred to as 'the Farm'.

Apart from the addition of two new water closets and the removal of the dung heap away from the living quarters, the most successful welfare project was the setting up of the Buckingham Palace Royal Mews School for the 'instruction of the children of servants belonging to the Royal Mews'. Established by the Queen in 1855, the school was maintained entirely at her own expense, and it succeeded for over two decades in giving what a school inspector called a 'useful and sensible education' to the children of the Mews.

Constantly changing governments had meant a quick succession of Masters of the Horse, and to give some continuity in the daily running of the Mews the permanent appointment of Crown Equerry was created in 1854. The first man to hold the post was a retired army officer, Major John Groves, formerly Essex Rifles. He was officially termed Crown Equerry, Secretary to the Master of the Horse and Superintendent of the Royal Stables. The title was designed to show that, although the office was held by a gentleman, his duties also included the clerical work required by the Master of the Horse. This menial aspect of his work meant he was not allowed through the doors of the Palace, and his orders were transmitted via the other equerries as the 'mode by which the orders for the Queen and the Royal Household are communicated to the Stables'.

Groves found himself in an unenviable position, with no social standing in the Palace and kept well below the salt by members of the Household and other equerries who were in personal attendance on the Queen. His position and duties were described in a letter from Sir Charles Phipps, Keeper of the Privy Purse, to the second Duke of Wellington, who was then Master of the Horse, as 'entirely distinct' and belonging 'exclusively to the Stables department'.

Groves did his best for his staff, but it was not until the year of his death in 1859 that an estimate was accepted to build forty new rooms above the coachhouses and stables around the quadrangle and back mews. These were added to the existing ninety-eight rooms, in which, much to the detriment of their health and working capacity, over one hundred and ninety-eight members of staff and their families had lived.

Colonel George Ashley Maude, Royal Artillery, a respected horseman and soldier, was Groves's successor. He took up residence in the newly built Crown Equerry's official home, an attractive house finished in 1858 to the west of the front gateway, corresponding with Nash's house for the Clerk of the Stables on the east side. Exceedingly deaf and blind in

The Master of the Horse, the fifteenth Earl of Westmorland (*right*), and the Crown Equerry, Lieutenant Colonel Seymour Gilbart-Denham, check a final detail with the Head Coachman before the carriage procession leaves the Mews for Victoria Station at the beginning of a state visit.

one eye, Maude was to remain in office for thirty-five years.

The grandson of a peer and with private means of his own, he remained unperturbed by courtiers who often considered his peremptory handling of Mews matters as overstepping the authority of his position. He campaigned successfully with the various government departments about the continual pension, medical and housing problems of his staff, and divided the joint post of Crown Equerry and Mews Superintendent into two separate offices. He also established the right to act without perpetual reference to the Master of the Horse, 'tho' he would of course report to him everything he does'. The Queen granted him direct access to discuss any aspect of the Royal Mews that he felt she should be aware of, and it became accepted that he was responsible for receiving and conveying the direct wishes of Her Majesty in any matters involving the Mews. These changes brought the Mews into line with other departments of the Household and provided the basis for the highly efficient organisation that has survived the last five reigns.

Maude was knighted in 1887, the year of the Golden Jubilee. When he died in his Mews house seven years later, the Queen felt she had lost a trusted friend, and noted in her journal of May 1894 that she was 'much grieved', for he had been 'a kind good man'.

During the fifty-two years of the next four reigns, although the village atmosphere remained, many aspects of the Royal Mews underwent considerable change. The arrival of the motor car and two world wars, as well as the constant demand for economy, rigorously curtailed the numbers of horses, men and carriages. Like any community, the Mews suffered its quota of wartime casualties and the departure of able-bodied men to fight. In the back mews a residents' medical ward was set up, coachhouses were turned into garages, single men were given their own dormitory, and continuous modernisation of the stables and married quarters took place overall.

After nearly a hundred years as a political appointment, in 1924 the office of Master of the Horse, together with those of Lord Chamberlain and Lord Steward, became permanent, non-political appointments as a result of a review of the Royal Household. The Master of the Horse remained in personal attendance upon the sovereign on state occasions, while the Crown Equerry continued as the executive head of the Mews.

Infallibly courteous in its dealings and always receptive to new ideas, the Pimlico Mews has come a long way since George III casually used the existing Buckingham House stables as an overflow for his horses and carriages.

2 The Mews Today

'It's like a small village which belongs to Buckingham Palace.'

Her Majesty The Queen in a TVS documentary,
'The Queen and Her Ceremonial Horses'

Under the Crown Equerry, the Royal Mews today is a tightly run department. Because of the nature of the job, many of the staff come from a military background.

In the original Nash offices, the Royal Mews Superintendent attends to discipline and welfare. Working closely with police and security, he has, amongst other duties, responsibility for co-ordinating the movements of the royal cars, horses and carriages at home and abroad.

He is assisted by the Comptroller of Stores, a part of whose job it is to obtain all the department's provisions and equipment. This means keeping a shrewd eye on the quality and price of the goods and services provided by contractors and suppliers. Details of his budgeting include the maintenance and replacement of liveries, harness and any contracted carriage repairs and restoration.

The Superintendent and Comptroller of Stores, working with a small office staff, the Head Chauffeur, the Head Coachman and the Head Carriage Restorer, keep the cars, carriages, horses and liveries to the very high standard that is required. The office also combines its daily routine with answering the continuous flow of mail containing enquiries from the general public.

Because of the shortage of stabling and schooling facilities for horses in London, by permission of The Queen the Mews offers its spare stables and the use of the riding school to the Civil Service Riding Club. In return the club provides on a 'use for keep' basis ponies for central London branches of Riding for the Disabled. The use of the school and private storage facilities are available to these groups five days of the working week. The school is also available to certain other organisations, including any mounted policemen who wish to school their horses.

With a few special exceptions, both chauffeurs and stable staff are expected to live on the job. The Mews complex accommodates families and single men and, where necessary, retirement homes are eventually found for staff at Hampton Court or Windsor.

The quadrangle is sadly no longer the safest of playgrounds, as private staff cars fill the spaces that once provided rounders and football pitches and a tennis court. As in every village, television (first brought into the Mews for The Queen's coronation) has supplanted the staff concerts and dance nights of the past. However, everybody knows everyone else and community life remains important in the Mews.

Many of the stable staff have generations of Mews or other royal employment behind them. Brothers, uncles, fathers, sons and cousins work among the senior and junior liveried helpers of today. Other men have a background of dealers' yards, the turf or the Army. Some are recruited from the King's Troop, Royal Horse Artillery, the Youth Opportunity Scheme, or, if suitable, are accepted on initiatives which vary from letters and telephone calls to enquiries at the office door.

Some applicants who have previously worked with horses are experienced in riding or driving when they arrive, while others have no previous knowledge but just a wish to work in the Mews. Probation is a six-month training period in riding, driving, pair driving and stable

Opposite The exercise brakes, painted in the royal livery colours of 'royal claret' and black lined in signal red, leave the Mews for Hyde Park most mornings. Put to pairs or teams, either coachman- or postilion-driven, they are used to instruct and train both men and horses.

management, during which time a certain standard must be reached. The days are past when extra weekly help was employed to clean the exercise harness, polish the brass, muck out and generally lend a hand. Nowadays the coachmen and all the liveried helpers share every aspect of stable work in the yard. State splendour may have its rewarding moments, but enthusiasm must also be retained for an unrelenting routine and an exacting job.

Since the reign of George III, a considerable number of documents has been kept concerning the Royal Mews. Many of the names, methods and expressions from the eighteenth century to be found in them are still in use in the Mews today, and are unknown outside. Memories remain vivid, nurtured by a mixture of knowledge, tradition and hearsay handed down by older members of staff.

There are joint ventures in carriage driving and displays with other European royal mews, and frequent exchanges of coachmen and grooms. Some successful candidates are sent for six months on the Army's long equitation course at Melton Mowbray.

Employment has always been found for men no longer fit to ride or drive. Carriages, harness, liveries and the yard need daily maintenance, and every ceremony benefits from extra liveried men as horse-holders, chockmen and attendants practised in Mews routine.

In accordance with Her Majesty's wishes and in consultation with the Crown Equerry, the Head Coachman co-ordinates the horses, men, livery, harness and carriages for every job or procession. Although there are obvious precedents, nothing is a fixture and everything is open to last-minute change. The ultimate decision will rest on the best presentation of Mews turnout applicable to a given situation.

Apart from state occasions and their attendant rehearsals, between eight and ten carriages a day can leave the Mews on various activities. Unless weather conditions are extremely adverse, one carriage that leaves the Mews twice a day every week is the Messenger Brougham. With the exception of Kensington Palace, the Brougham is used to collect and deliver internal mail and messages between the other royal households and their offices. The carriage can also call on errands at Coutts Bank, Horse Guards and several other destinations nearby.

The potential of the light and manageable one-horse continental street cab was noted by Lord Brougham in the late 1830s. A man of exceptional enthusiasm and energy, he imported a cab from Paris and persuaded the coachbuilding firm of Robinson & Cook to copy it for him. Although not immediately successful, eventually broughams were widely used, often changed and adapted to their owners' personal specifications.

In the Royal Mews, a brougham is essentially a single-horse carriage, lined in leather and with room for two passengers. Apart from the first three years of the Second World War, when the messenger run was curtailed, Mews broughams have been in daily use since 1843. The one in most constant use today is painted and lined in blue, put to either a bay or grey with the driver in plain livery.

Modern traffic conditions require an exceptional horse and a relaxed man on the box. Before being passed out to drive on his own, a new liveried helper will undergo a month or so of instruction with a qualified

The horses and stable staff are organised into four groups referred to as 'sets'. These comprise four men, each usually with a pair of horses to look after. An experienced coachman has charge of each complete set and, working under the Head Coachman, he is responsible for the direction and the achievements of his men and horses.

man beside him. After that he will be tested by one of the senior coachmen who will decide whether or not the required standard has been reached.

The messenger and his packages are collected from Buckingham Palace and, while the messenger dictates the round, the driver chooses the route. Apart from the usual traffic regulations, the Brougham, which according to the head messenger can get around Trafalgar Square 'quicker than a bus', maintains a fair trotting pace to keep its place in the traffic.

Young horses being schooled to traffic are often paired with an experienced horse and driven in a clarence. This is another utility vehicle, slightly larger than a brougham, and there are several in the Mews. Drawn by two horses, with a coachman and carriage groom on the box, a clarence seats four passengers and was generally considered to be an excellent family town carriage.

According to rank and seniority, members of the Royal Household and staff were in the past allowed the use of either a brougham or a clarence for making general calls or to go shopping.

Opposite Smokeless fuel is used now in the forge built by Prince Albert in 1840. Horseshoes are always made in either front or hind pairs. Finished sets for individual horses are named and hung on the forge wall.

Throughout the year on special dates that celebrate among other things The Queen's accession, her coronation and the birthdays of her immediate family, a single royal claret brougham is used for the twice-daily messenger run. The coachman wears scarlet livery in the summer and a drab coat with a gold-laced top hat in the winter. Here the brougham stops outside the Privy Purse Door of Buckingham Palace to collect the messenger.

The Bow-Fronted Clarence, made by Clark & Co of Aberdeen at the turn of the nineteenth century.

The interior of the Clarence is lined with deep-buttoned black leather upholstery stuffed with horsehair. It has a plain box-cloth ceiling and painted bone clasps on the window and door pulls. The bow window at the front can be opened by sliding it back on either side.

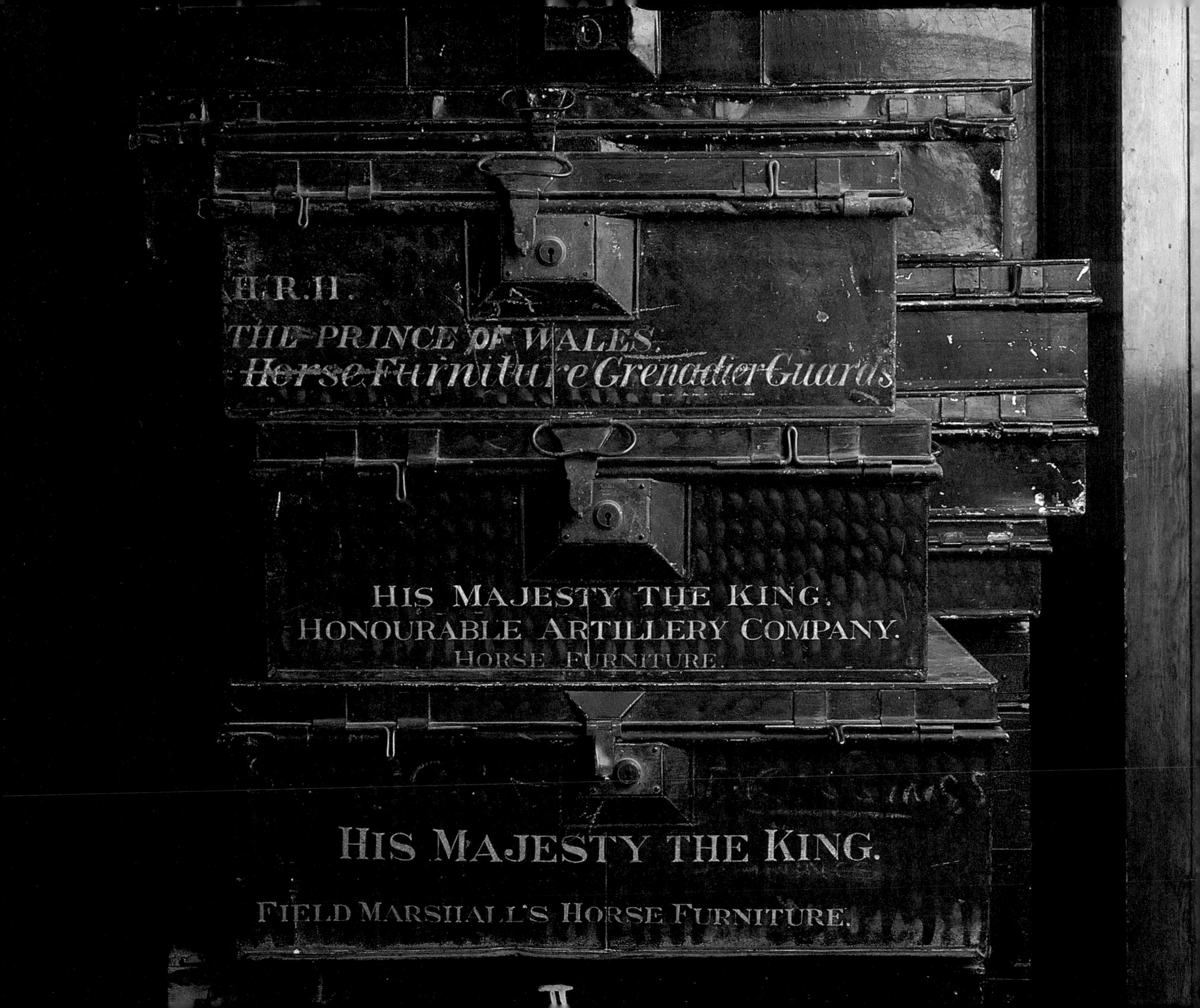
H.R.H.
THE PRINCE OF WALES.
Horse Furniture Grenadier Guards
HIS MAJESTY THE KING.
HONOURABLE ARTILLERY COMPANY.
HORSE FURNITURE.
HIS MAJESTY THE KING.
FIELD MARSHALL'S HORSE FURNITURE.

VEHICLE		LOCATION	DATE	COMPLETED
Nº 11 EXERCISE BRAKE	REFURBISHED	A.S.BRIDGES	26 FEB	
7 SMALL 4 LARGE BOSSES 1 LAMP				
ASCOT Nº 5	REHOODING.	MEWS/CHAPMAN	JULY	
SEMI-STATE Nº2.	CUT SHUT REPAINT WHEELS	CROFORDS	JAN	
IRISH STATE COACH	REFURBISHED	MEWS	21 JUNE '88	H
" " "	ALL LEATHER WORK	LUXFORD	30 JUNE '88	
" " "	LAMP/WHEELS	CROFORDS	29 JUNE 88	
" " "	LEATHER TOP	MEWS/CHAPMANS	JULY	
STATE LANDAU Nº 5	REFURBISH INTERIOR	" "	"	
" " Nº 7	" "	" "	"	
GLASS COACH	REPAIR SEAT	" "	"	

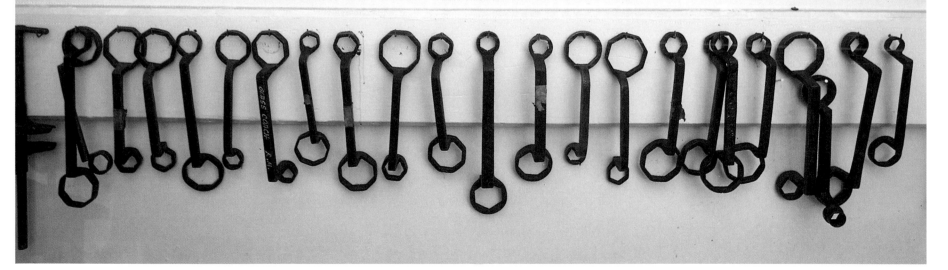

Above Co-ordination between the Mews carriage restorers and outside craftsmen, wheelwrights and harness makers are noted on the Paint Shop blackboard.

Opposite Equipment in the Mews is carefully labelled and stored.

Above Removing stable stains from the grey team required for an early-morning rehearsal can mean an even earlier start than the detailed time of 0400 hours.

Opposite Early-morning rehearsals before an incoming state visit, the Opening of Parliament or any other occasion are a carefully planned and important part of Mews routine.

Above When several carriages are used, it is customary for the Queen's Bargemaster and Royal Watermen to do extra duty as carriage footmen.

Royal Watermen were first mentioned in records from the fourteenth century when the River Thames was the main highway through London. By Queen Victoria's reign these appointments had become mere sinecures. It was King George V who stipulated that his 'bargemaster and twenty-three' should revert to being working river men, and this remains a condition of today's appointments.

The Bargemaster wears white hose and a tail coat.

Over page Coachmen's state whips used today at the Opening of Parliament and on other major state occasions.

Formerly whips were issued as postilions' and coachmen's personal property. Their quality was determined by seniority and use. The Head Coachman's state four-horse whip was mounted with silver gilt ornaments and engraved with his name.

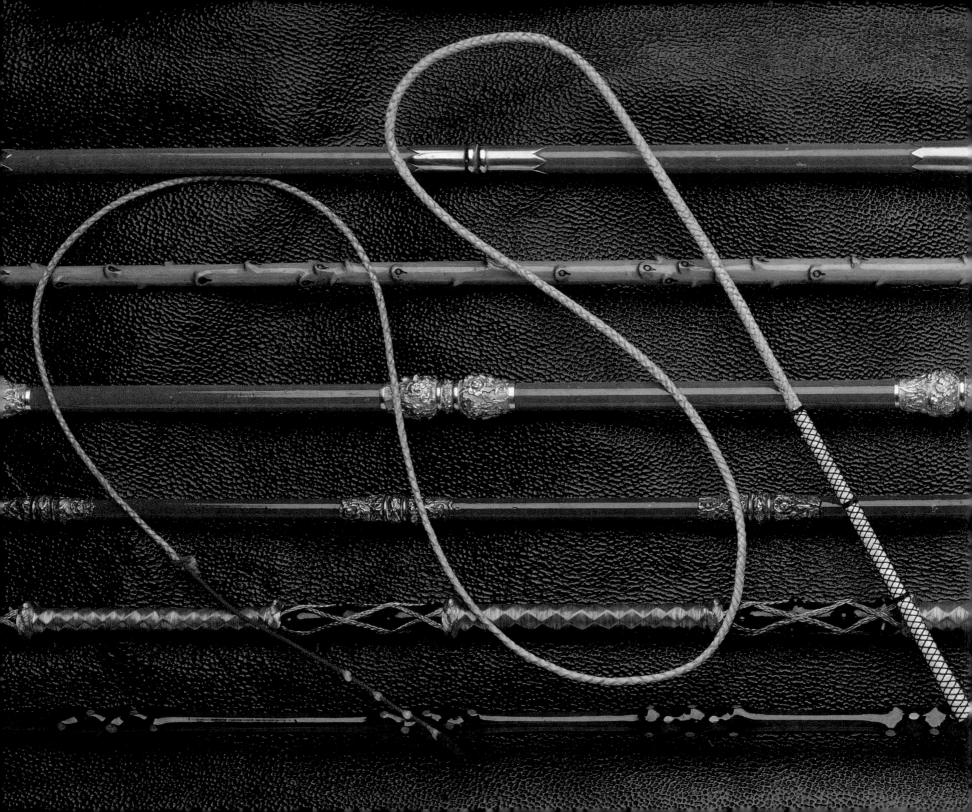

Above   The State Coach in the Mews today. An entry in the day book kept by the Clerk of the Stables for 24 November 1762 records that, 'This morning about five o'clock the new state coach was brought to the mews: and about 8 o'clock eight of the creams [cream stallions] were put to it in order to try it round the mews, when it was found to go well and to be fit for use.'

Previous page   Detail of a painting attributed to John Wootton (1686–1764) of King George III's procession to the Houses of Parliament. It was probably painted to record the first public appearance of the new State Coach on 25 November 1762.

In his day book for that year, the Clerk of the Stables records, 'The mob was exceedingly great; yet no other accident happened, but one of the door glasses and the handle of the door being broke.' He also remarked on the first use of the new state harness, the horses being 'ornamented with blue ribbon and Morocco trappings'.

3 The Gold State Coach, 1762

'There is come forth a new State Coach which
has cost £8,000. It is a beautiful object . . .'

Horace Walpole to Sir Horace Mann,
30 November 1762

As much of London was gradually rebuilt after the Great Fire of 1666, many of its streets were widened and paved for the first time, and so became suitable for horse-drawn traffic. Until then regular travel there by private or hired carriage had been impractical and a public nuisance. In 1677 King Charles II granted a joint charter that formally recognised the existing guilds of coach builders and coach harness makers, and this marked the beginning of a boom in coach building that would continue for over two hundred years.

Outside the major cities, roads were still quagmires for much of the year, and it was not until the end of the eighteenth century that any notable improvements in this situation took place. Until then, even for the rich, travelling by coach in the country was a doubtful pleasure, and the coach-building trade concentrated on making town vehicles as status symbols for the rich.

On his accession in 1760, King George III ordered a 'very superb' state coach to be built for his wedding to Princess Charlotte of Mecklenburg-Strelitz and for his coronation. In fact, the vehicle was ready for neither: it was not seen in public until 25 November 1762 when, according to the *Annual Register*, 'His Majesty went to the House of Peers, to open the session of Parliament'. Public anticipation was immense and newspapers reported that several rooms in and near Parliament Square were taken by ladies and gentlemen 'paying two guineas (£2.10p) each to see His Majesty pass to the House in his new state coach'.

Although it was by then customary to commission architects, sculptors and artists to help design and decorate elaborate coaches, few of the King's subjects had ever seen anything resembling the grandeur of the new one. However, although Horace Walpole recorded in a letter to a friend that it was 'thought to be the finest ever built', he pointed out that the coach was 'crowded with improprieties'. Many felt that the conqueror's emblems and trophies of war which covered it alluded rather prematurely to victory in the Seven Years War with France, which did not end until the following year, and the massive sea tritons that supported the body 'not very well adapted to pulling a land carriage'. For the most part, however, the coach made a triumphant debut and nearly two hundred and thirty years later it still remains in the Royal Mews.

The design of the State Coach, according to the day book of George III's Clerk of the Stables, is a composition of several 'drawings made for the purpose' and 'thrown into one' by the King's former drawing master, William Chambers, surveyor of His Majesty's Board of Works. Supervised by the Duke of Rutland, then Master of the Horse, and Chambers, it was built in the London workshops of Samuel Butler, a future Master of the Coachbuilders' Company.

The coach is twelve feet high and twice as long. After tax, the final cost, which included an appropriate set of state harness, was £7,652.16s.9½d, an enormous sum of money for those days. The largest fee for work on the coach was £2,500 which was paid to the sculptor Joseph Wilton, third keeper of the Royal Academy, for the immense amount of intricate carving involved. Wilton's assistant was the young Florentine artist and engraver Giovanni Battista Cipriani, who for £315 painted eight side panels with allegorical scenes portraying England's greatness.

King George III's State Coach has always required eight horses to draw it. Because of its weight and suspension, it is only used at a walking pace in a ceremonial procession.

Lions' heads support the four corner palm trees. These are laden with trophies of war and in turn support the roof of the coach.

Gilded dolphins hold in place the intricately carved splinter bar by which the coach is drawn. The buckles on the red morocco leather straps are water gilt.

SALMON & GLUCKSTEIN'S
CIGARETTES

THE STATE
COACH

CORONATION 1911.

As King George IV elected to walk to his coronation, the coach was first used for this ceremony by his brother King William IV.

It remained in constant use for all great state ceremonies until 1861, but after the Prince Consort's death Queen Victoria rebelled against its 'distressing oscillations' and the coach was stored until the accession of her son King Edward VII. It is shown here on a cigarette card dating from King George V's coronation in 1911.

Opposite Judged strictly as paintings, the eight panels by Cipriani are not of exceptional quality. They are, however, an important part of the coach as a whole and many hours have been spent on their repair and maintenance.

The back panel shows Neptune and Amphitrite with their attendants bringing the tributes of the world to the British shore.

Below Before the coronation of King Edward VII in 1902, the coach was extensively renovated by Hooper. To give a clearer view of Their Majesties the coachman's box seat was removed and the vehicle has since then been drawn by four postilion pairs. Hooper introduced a strong braking system, which is hand-worked by the liveried brakeman who walks between the back wheels. These changes are evident in this model which was made for the coronation of the present Queen.

The three cherubs holding the crown and regalia represent the genii of England, Scotland and Ireland.

During preparations for King Edward VII's coronation, the Master of the Horse, the Duke of Portland, dreamt that the coach stuck while passing under Horse Guards arch and the crown had to be cut from the roof. On waking, he ordered a new set of measurements to be taken and found that repairs under the arch had raised the road level and reduced the clearance by two feet, an error that had to be promptly rectified.

The coach was regularly used by King George V to travel to the State Opening of Parliament. King Edward VIII, however, never used it, for when he opened Parliament in 1936 the day was wet and the procession was changed to motor cars.

This collector's cut-out model of the coach was sold in a souvenir booklet for the present Queen's coronation in 1953.

A gold bracelet charm.

After storage during the Second World War, preparations to overhaul the coach were put in hand by King George VI. The wheels, copied from an ancient triumphal chariot, had warped badly and complex trials took place before a method was devised for bonding rubber on to the antique iron tyres.

The work of artists, jewellers and model-makers over the years has helped to make the State Coach almost as well known a symbol of the British monarchy as the Crown itself.

Although the coach has had constant attention paid to its upkeep during the last two hundred and twenty-nine years, the Jubilee of 1977 was the first time in its history that the entire vehicle was regilded.

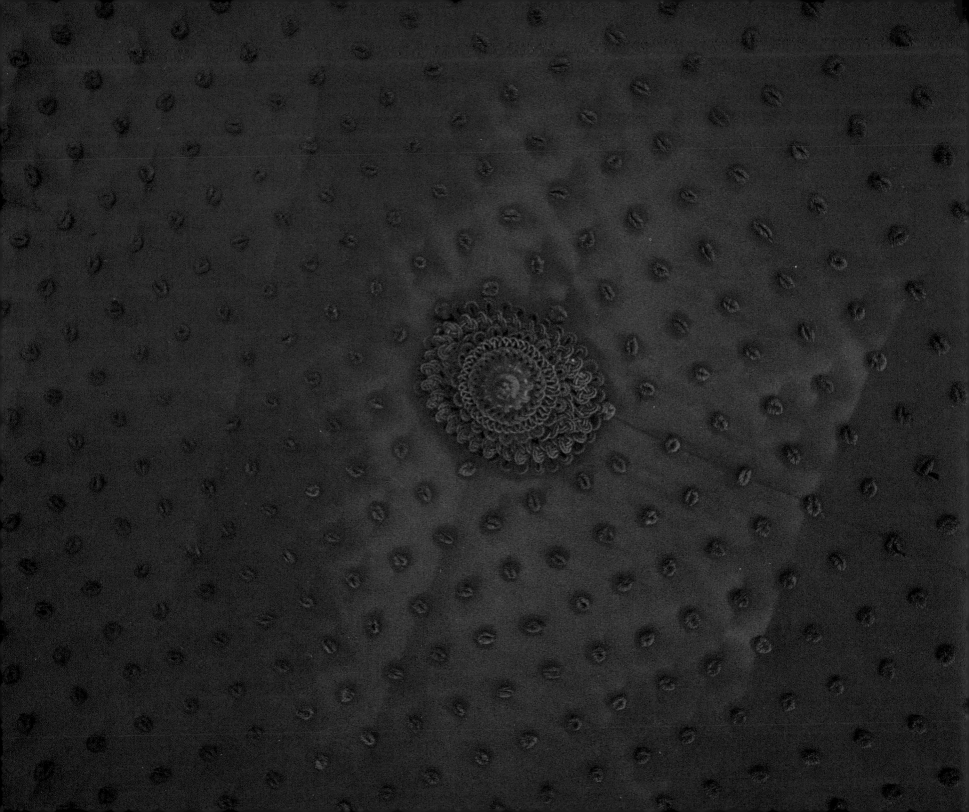

Above Inside the State Coach. After the coronation ceremony the weight
of the Sceptre is supported in a socket near the armrest. The Orb in the
Sovereign's hand rests on a small table inserted into the socket on the other
side.

Last refurbished in 1902, the interior was partly re-upholstered for The
Queen's Silver Jubilee procession in 1977. Twenty metres of specially
woven material dyed to match the original fabric were used.

Opposite   The roof lining inside the State Coach. Interior lighting under the roof was installed at the time of Queen Elizabeth II's coronation.

A stamp to celebrate The Queen's Silver Jubilee.

Any procession involving the State Coach is essentially a walking procession. Overall the vehicle weighs four tons and, described by one member of the Mews staff as 'all right when it gets going', travels at around 3 mph.

A 'side' of the red moroccan state harness that was used for The Queen's Jubilee procession.

The complete set of eight sides of moroccan state harness in use today was made for King William IV, when the Royal Arms still bore the white horse of Hanover. Between 1861 and 1939 some of the other moroccan sets were used on appropriate occasions with a postilion-driven landau.

Since the war, the harness has only been seen with the State Coach. It was completely overhauled and renovated by Turner-Bridgar, harness makers to The Queen, before being used for the Silver Jubilee.

At least five sets of state harness for the coach have been made since 1762. The eight sides that make up each set are made from moroccan leather, all similar in style and weight, with gilt ormolu buckles and ornaments. The harness is breast harness, dyed red or blue, though after her coronation Queen Victoria had a set made that had both colours in it. Although there is only one complete set of eight sides still in use today, which is in red, various sides and pieces from previous sets can still be found in the Mews.

The Royal Arms used on the Prince Regent's harness shows his label as Heir Apparent in the top centre of the shield and round the unicorn's neck (*top right*).

Above During his regency (1811–20) George IV had both red and blue sets of harness made. This pad weighs 25 lbs.

When mounted with the bit and bridoon, each bridle weighs 18 lbs. A full side, which includes the bridle but not the postilion's saddle, weighs about 110 lbs.

Over page Two hundred and fifteen years after its first appearance, Her Majesty The Queen is driven in the Gold State Coach to the thanksgiving service in St Paul's Cathedral to celebrate her Silver Jubilee on 7 June 1977. It was thought that the journey was the furthest the coach had ever travelled. Careful trials were carried out beforehand, including a midnight rehearsal along the ceremonial route to test how well the coach stood up to the strain of going up and down Ludgate Hill.

4 The Carriage Horses

'The blacks can be used if The Queen wishes it,
but are in the same category as the creams,
being all stallions and have never been considered Queen's horses.'

Letter from Colonel Maude to Sir Henry
Ponsonby, 17 March 1887

Until the arrival of the internal combustion engine, draught horses were regarded by many people as little more than an expendable necessity. Between three and six years was the average work span of a coach horse on the road, after which even the horses of the aristocracy passed through the dealers' and knackers' yards, sold on to customers seeking further mileage at a knock-down price. By contrast, the town work of state carriage horses guaranteed them a longer and easier life as well as providing the public with a lavish display.

When the Elector of Hanover succeeded to the English throne in 1714 as King George I, he imported as his state carriage horses the cream stallions formerly kept for the exclusive use of his family in Hanover. The King later bred from these at Hampton Court, the traditional home of the Royal Stud, and horses of this type remained in use for most of the next century. However, when George III learned that Napoleon had dared to use his family's cream horses after the French seizure of Hanover, he ordered that in future only an imported breed of black stallion should be used with the English royal carriages. This lasted until Napoleon's defeat in 1815, after which both cream and black stallions were used in the Royal Mews until after the First World War.

In the early 1920s it was decided to dispense with the creams, who were proving difficult to breed and impossible to obtain elsewhere. Both they and the blacks – described as 'sulky brutes' by the Master of the Horse, the Duke of Portland – were displaced in the Mews by bay carriage horses until, in the 1930s, King George V (1910–36) started putting grey horses to his two leading carriages in any procession. The name 'Windsor Grey' by which these horses have since become known refers not to a specific breed but dates from the removal by King Edward VIII (1936) of the grey carriage horses – which had previously been stabled at Windsor – to the London Mews.

The Mews carriage horses vary in height from 16.2 hands to over 17 hands, and their present number is based on keep for thirty. The greys kept for Her Majesty's use usually number ten and are either home bred or come from a number of different sources that include Holland, Ireland and Germany. The twenty bays are predominantly Cleveland bays with an increasing number of a Cleveland–Oldenburg cross bred at the Royal Stud, Hampton Court. The grey horses are formed into one set while the bays are divided by size into two sets. There is a fourth set of new and young horses under the direction of the Rough Rider who, with the Head Coachman, is responsible for their schooling and training. Buying in young animals already broken to harness is not always successful and, in a job where temperament is of the utmost importance, there is growing support for training the homebred horses from scratch. There are also benefits from early schooling sessions with bands, flags, balloons and simulated crowd nuisances.

Opposite The public on open days see The Queen's carriage horses stabled in the nineteenth-century State Stable, originally the home of the cream and black stallions. Several of the other buildings have since had stalls converted into loose boxes and it is in these that the horses are kept when they are not on display. Here the horses are shown pillar-reined, as they would be for any special private visit.

The young horses are first broken to the saddle before being introduced gradually to harness. If they prove suitable they are put into appropriate sets to gain further experience working alongside older horses.

The general stable routine is based around the Head Coachman's daily detail; it includes at least 'one hour's good exercise and more for horses that need it' before every ceremonial duty. One early-morning schooling exercise for novice men and horses is the driving of some of the larger carriages through and around the arches between the Buckingham Palace forecourt and quadrangle.

Except for the thoroughbred Cleveland bays already registered by the Stud, the horses are named by Her Majesty. Once the decision has been made to keep them each horse is given two nameplates painted with its name and year of birth. One nameplate is kept with the horse wherever it happens to be stabled, while the other is permanently hung over its stall in the State Stable at the end of the Royal Mews quadrangle.

Most of the horses will be turned out for up to six weeks at the end of the summer season. Modern methods of feeding, bedding and veterinary treatment keep many of them in work until they are into their twenties, thus providing Her Majesty with experienced veterans of great quality.

Mane laying and dressing is only used on special occasions and has remained unchanged since the eighteenth century.
The colour of the ribbon has varied throughout history in accordance with the sovereign's choice.

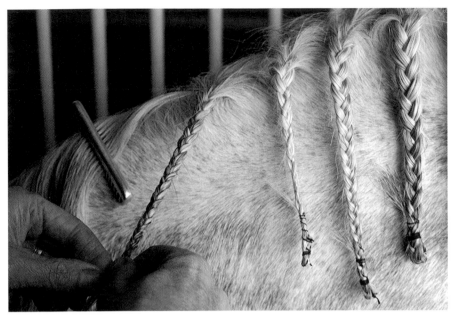

As many plaits as possible are put in, although the mane is left loose under the collar.

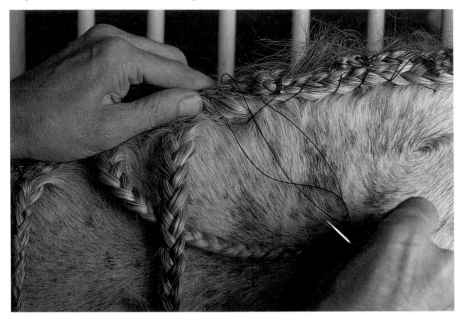

The individual plaits are laid down the neck and stitched in.

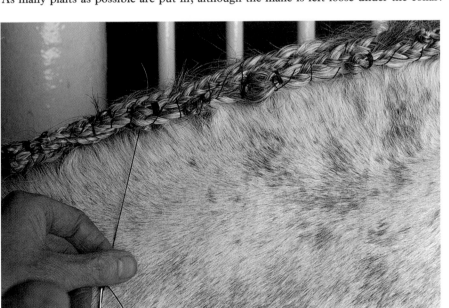

It is important that this part of the work is as firm and tight as possible.

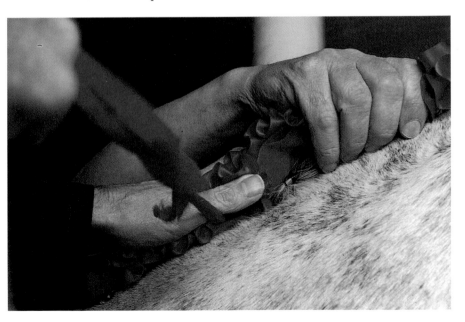

Two pairs of hands are now essential.

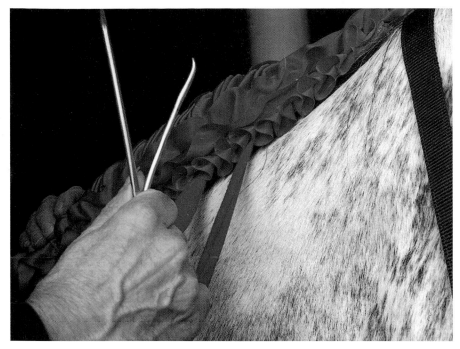

Working from the withers, the laces of the mane lay are drawn through both sides of the plaited mane.

The bridle is put on.

The ends of the two laces are tied to the screw on top of the headpiece to which the matching state ear bows are already attached.

The traditional three rosettes already sewn on to the rest of the mane dressing are then tied with tape through and under the mane lay.

Above 'It's the hardest thing in the business to get four horses to go with their heads nice and straight,' says Head Coachman Arthur Showell.

Opposite Once the mane lay is firmly in place, the final dressing can be attached to fall on either the nearside or offside of a pair of horses. Oscar, a sixteen-year-old Dutch gelding, has had his mane dressed to fall on the offside.

63

Four sets of state harness – the Black Horse, the Town Coach, the Square Buckle and the Council – being used as posting (ride and lead) harness during a state visit.

Although there has been a constant programme of repair and releathering, all the brasswork is nineteenth-century.

5 Harness and Horse Trappings

'Had a proper State Harness room been provided,
as unquestionably it ought to have been,
when this mews was built . . .'

Master of the Horse, the Earl of Albemarle,
7 February 1834

There is no doubt that the fourth Earl of Albemarle would be highly relieved to see the care with which the state harness is now kept in its own well-appointed harness room. Apart from the red moroccan harness used only with the State Coach, there are seven other sets of black leather state harness, each identified by a different name.

Each of the seven sets is made up of six sides and can be broken down and used for every combination of team, pair driving and postilion work. A four-in-hand team was not formerly considered a town or ceremonial turn-out, and if six horses were put to a coachman-driven vehicle, the leading pair were postilion-ridden.

The seven sets in use were made during the nineteenth century, and they are thought to form the finest collection in existence. The difference in weight of the individual sides that make up each separate set varies from 56 lbs to 112 lbs, making some sets more suitable than others for use with young or inexperienced horses.

Teams of horses are matched not only in terms of colour, temperament and height but also in length. Adapting harness made for stallions and the heavier animals used in the past requires very knowledgeable fitting if the horses are not to become sore from unnecessary rubbing.

There is a regular system of renovation and replacement, using leather which has been specially dressed during the tanning stage to ensure greater durability. Parts of the harness are still hand-stitched with the traditional 15–18 stitches per inch.

Over twenty-five sides can be required for a state ceremony, each of which must be taken completely to pieces, washed down, cleaned and polished before being used again.

A side of Black Horse harness. The Black Horse harness was probably made for the coronation procession of King William IV. Each side weighs approximately 112 lbs and the armorial ornaments bear the white horse of Hanover. Contemporary paintings and later photographs show that, until their dispersal in the 1920s, the black stallions were turned out in this harness.

Bridles used with the Black Horse harness and the Queen's harness weigh 16 lbs.

To prevent the heavy bridles slipping forward over the horses' heads, comfortably fitted bearing reins are used with the state harness.

The Town Coach harness is easily recognised by the heavy chasing of rose, thistle and shamrock on the brasswork. The harness was made in the early years of Queen Victoria's reign and was the first set to bear the altered Royal Arms. As a woman could not rule in Hanover, Queen Victoria removed the German arms from the Royal Coat of Arms.

Three sets of harness are referred to by the shape of their buckles: the Fluted Buckle, the Square Buckle and the Round Buckle. The bridle shown here is of Fluted Buckle harness.

Crowned terrets on a pad of Fluted Buckle harness.

The old method of rubbing in acid-free charcoal dust is used to clean away traces of metal polish from the leather around the more ornate pieces of brass.

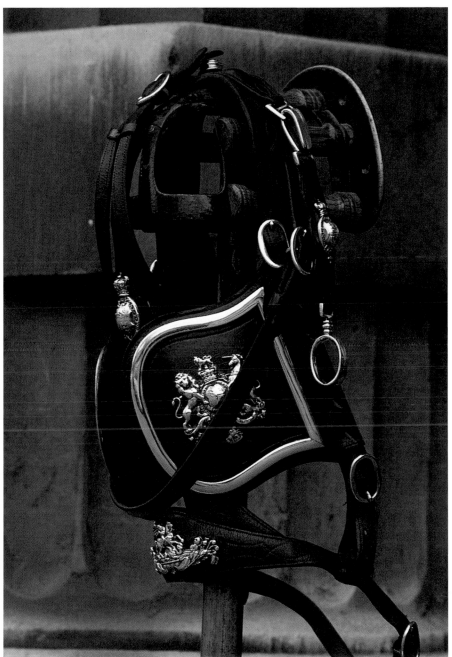

Square Buckle and Round Buckle harness. The Round Buckle is the lightest set and used on the young horses.

The Council set is also relatively light; each side weighs around 71 lbs.

Bridles are not mounted with bits until the day before they are used. The state bits are buxton bits with a royal boss on the side. Each horse's mouth is individually bitted.

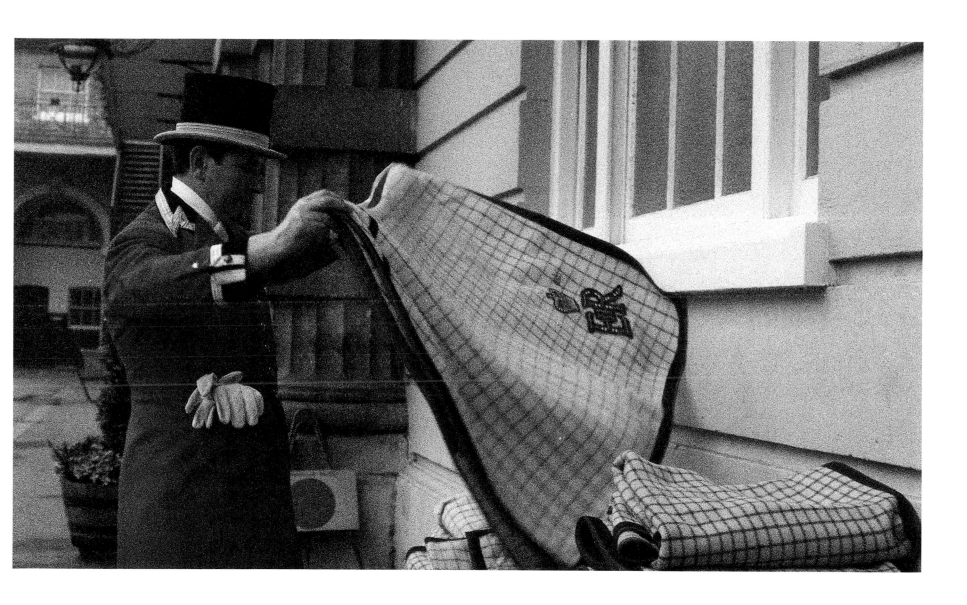

The royal cyphers on the best day rugs and quarter sheets are hand embroidered.

The state earbows and rosettes used for the grey team. The earbows and fronts (browbands) are unwound, washed and rewound by hand after use. As Sir George Maude remarked in 1889, 'Ribbon is a very expensive item and quickly deteriorates.'

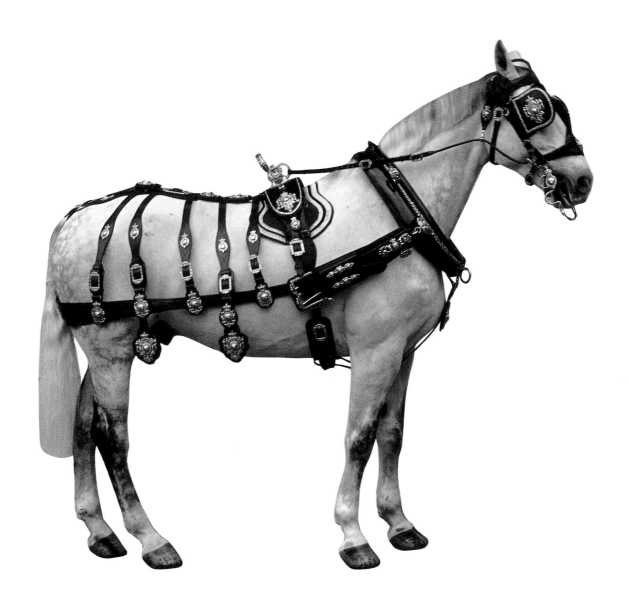

Twilight, a ten-year-old Hanoverian gelding, turned out in the Number 3 state harness known as the Queen's harness. This set of harness was ordered by King William IV in 1836. The six sides cost £115 and were paid for out of the Privy Purse. The harness is generally used with whichever state carriage Her Majesty is being driven in. Outriders in front of carriages are mounted on horses of the same colour as those put to the vehicle. Harness appointments for outriders complement the set used on the carriage horses.

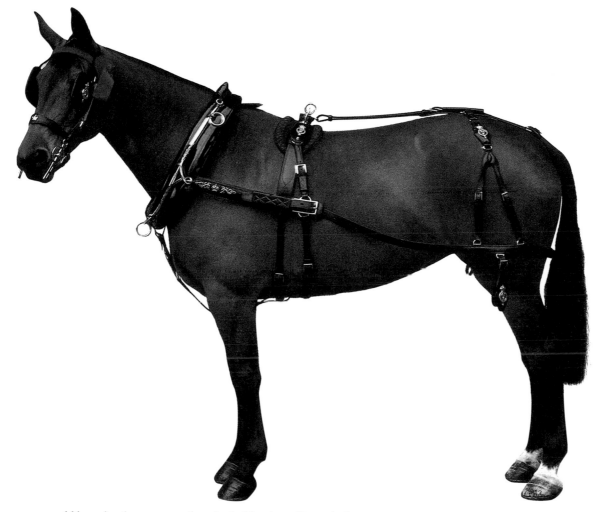

Above Honey Buzzard, a seven-year-old homebred mare, turned out in the Number 1 Barouche harness. The mare's breeding is by Spartacus out of Osprey, a Cleveland-Oldenburg cross.

Over page Twenty-four sides of Ascot posting harness, three pairs of Ambassador driving harness, two pairs of Barouche harness and several other sets of show and driving harness are kept in the Ascot Harness Room in the back mews.

In the picture Ascot posting harness is put up on the left with the Ambassador driving harness on the right. Postilions now use the modern saddles in the foreground.

Spares of appropriate harness are taken out on every job.

77

Rosettes are added as required to the fronts of the bridles. Outriders' bridles are mounted with rosettes on both sides.

6 The Livery

'The *standing* footmen with the six dress landaus
will be in State liveries like the coachmen,
plush and silk stockings.'

Letter from Colonel Maude to Sir Henry Ponsonby,
2 February 1887

In the fifteenth century 'livery' simply referred to the provision of a servant's food, clothing, lodging, and fodder for his horse if one was provided. 'Maintenance', on the other hand, implied the employer's protection of such a servant, should any transgression of the law, financial or otherwise, occur while on his master's business. A liveried man wore his master's badge as proof that this support would be forthcoming. Gradually, clothing on which the badge was worn became more distinctive and in time the word 'livery' came to mean the special garments worn by servants of a particular household.

Georgian town and state livery echoed the Hanoverian delight in all details of uniform and ceremonial dress. Since aristocratic society revolved around the court it became a point of honour for the fashionable to have their carriages, horses, harness and servants turned out to standards of bewildering grandeur. Different liveries were required at different times of the day, often worn by footmen chosen more for their height and the shapeliness of their legs than their abilities as servants.

Tailors patronised by royalty and the nobility became the livery tailors to their households, with every nuance of rank below stairs indicated by the quantity of buttons, capes, lace and decoration shown on the immaculate garments.

Livery designs in the late eighteenth century were partly copied from the current fashions of the road. Coachmen, whose skill and knowledge of horseflesh gave them a superiority beyond class distinction, were admired by young aristocrats who aspired to drive their own elegant turnouts and aped the coachmen's flamboyance of dress.

Post boys, who had formerly delivered the mail on horseback, were now maintained by the network of posting inns throughout the countryside. Their job was to ride the nearside horse of a pair while leading the offside one. Extra pairs of horses driven this way were often added as additional draught to a tired team. Teams put to private coaches were changed at the inns whose postilions drove the new team and later brought the horses back. The practical uniform of the post boys became the postilion livery of the aristocracy. Their short tight jackets, set off by top boots and a tall hat, were covered in bad weather by a coat of drab box cloth, slit to the waist and long enough to cover the rider's thighs. The smaller the man, the smarter he was deemed to be, and in private service an elegant set of liveried postilions working as a team was as much commented upon as the horses they handled.

Apart from a few details, Her Majesty's livery in the Royal Mews has changed little since the eighteenth century. Although, historically, a sum of money has always been set aside each year for replacements, to have a new Full State livery coat made now is very rare indeed. Wherever possible men are fitted out from the stores, and only measured up for essential items.

As well as Full State livery each man must, on certain occasions, wear either a scarlet, black or drab frock coat. Used with kneebreeches, breeches and boots, or black trousers, depending on the order of dress required, these traditional livery coats are worn when driving, riding or on the ground.

Postilions also wear dark blue Semi-State jackets as well as Ascot livery; plain black undress postilion livery is sometimes worn, and everyone has one black and one gold-laced top hat that bears a royal cockade.

Modern stable dress, with well fitting riding hats and serviceable coats and breeches, is worn for everyday exercise, while the dress for all formal duty is set out in the Head Coachman's daily detail.

By tradition, only the sovereign's coachman wore a cap, a custom which ensured him instant recognition. Since the 1960s the Queen's coachman has worn a tricorn hat with Full State livery like the other coachmen, although her carriage footmen still wear caps.

Bicorn hats and swords are worn by footmen on the other carriages.

Formerly there was a significant difference between the number of rows of curls on the Head Coachman's wig and those of the other coachmen.

Breeches with buttons dating from the reign of King Edward VII are not uncommon amongst the livery. Blue plush breeches with white stockings are worn by footmen and coachmen on Semi-State occasions, while red plush breeches are worn with specially dyed pink stockings when Full State livery is used.

A coachman's Full State driving coat and waistcoat weigh 16 lbs.

Horses have scant appreciation of history, and livery receives a fair amount of natural punishment. Garments are returned to the livery tailors for major alterations and repairs, but otherwise all livery is maintained in the stores. Here, surrounded by a fascinating part of Mews history, the storeman continues to mark new names into many of the garments under the names of men who were once employed by Queen Victoria.

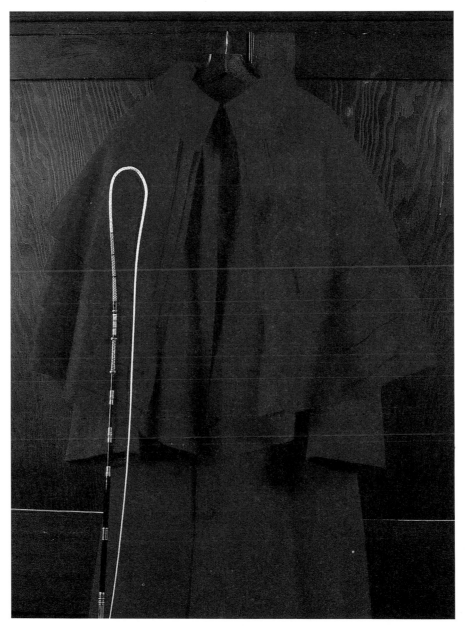

The traditional coachmen's wrappers were originally designed by a tailor called Benjamin as effective top garments for the men who drove the mail coaches in all weathers.

Red wrappers have been part of the royal livery since the reign of King George III and are still worn by coachmen in wet or cold weather. Each wrapper requires eleven metres of double-width material and hours of skilful cutting. A footman's red wrapper has only two capes.

A walking groom's coat and waistcoat made in the reign of Queen Victoria.

In a state walking procession, two grooms walk outside each pair of horses. The crook of the walking stick is used when necessary to pick up the slack of the traces as the coach turns.

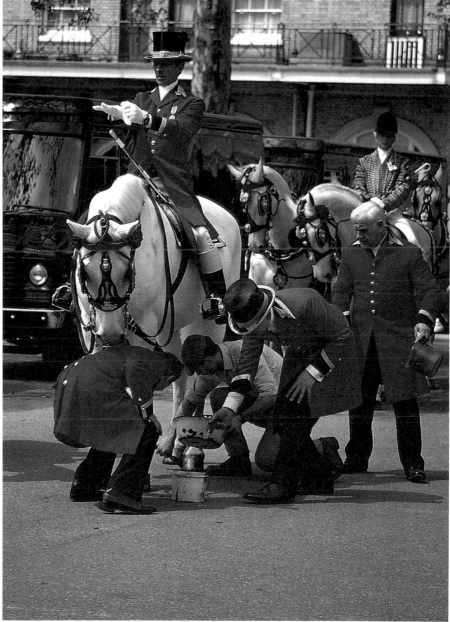

The postilions' curls are traditional and their wigs are professionally re-curled when necessary. The wigs require extremely short haircuts underneath them.

A gold-laced hat is always worn with scarlet livery.

An outrider in front of Her Majesty's carriage prepares to leave the Mews quadrangle before a state visit. The 'thrushes' tongue' detail on the scarlet livery collar has been retained from the eighteenth century.

LINEN. № 2.

Above   Full State postilion jackets have over 41 metres of gold lace and tubular braid applied to them.

Opposite   Weeks of work and untold hours of tailoring apprenticeship lie behind a new Ascot postilion livery. Laying on the lace on the lancer front is a skilled accomplishment in itself. Ascot livery, based on the royal racing colours, is worn by all postilions throughout the Royal Ascot meeting. By tradition, the livery is also used on other ceremonial occasions when Full State livery would be inappropriate.

This illustration from a Royal Mews livery book of 1887 shows the differences then in the height between postilions, footmen and outriders. Today there is no such distinction between them. The dark blue postilion jacket and gold-laced hat is termed today Semi-State livery.

Traditionally a pistol was attached to the end of the travelling cord worn across the footman's scarlet coat. Footmen in attendance on carriages no longer wear boots and buckskin breeches, but all postilions and outriders wear top boots, whose tops are kept a uniform colour with a specially prepared mixture of leather dressing.

On the second day of a state visit, carriages with postilions in Semi-State livery wait in St James's Palace garden while a visiting head of state receives High Commissioners for the Commonwealth countries and ambassadors accredited to the Court of St James. The footmen are wearing blue plush breeches with white stockings and buckled shoes.

A postilion wears a leather-covered iron leg guard (*second left*) strapped around the outside of his right boot to stop his leg being crushed by the pole between the two horses.

Although the convention is not always observed in practice, the wearing of a cockade is properly restricted to servants of the Royal Family, or the servants of those who by implication serve the Crown such as judges or army officers. The black cockade worn by the Royal Mews liveried servants was introduced in the reign of King George I and denotes service to the House of Hanover. They are circular and very distinctive.

Drab coats are worn in cold weather for riding, driving or on the ground.

Although footmen no longer powder their hair, the black rosette at the back of the coat was to stop the powder from spoiling the gold lace on the collar around the nape of the neck.

7 Royal Carriages

'A carriage is a complex production.
From one point of view it is a piece of mechanism,
from another, a work of art.'

Henry Julian, in a paper read to the Institute of British Carriage Manufacturers,
29 April 1884

By 1786, roads outside the towns had improved to such an extent that the post office discontinued the use of mounted post boys and started a delivery system with scheduled coaches. The English countryside first saw the royal carriage livery colours when the 'mail' thundered into every corner of the land. These coaches were all identical, painted in deep claret and black with scarlet wheels and undercarriages. The bodywork carried a royal cypher on the door and the four great orders of chivalry on the quarter panels.

With better road surfaces and carriage suspension, sophisticated carriages could now be used outside the towns, and the coachbuilding trade flourished. In spite of the growing nineteenth-century network of railways and canals, travelling carriages remained popular. Road vehicles were still necessary for short journeys and between departure points, railway stations and final destinations, while in the towns the state and dress vehicles of the wealthy and the lesser carriages needed for both public and private use meant a steady increase in the volume of road traffic.

During the early years of Queen Victoria's reign, English coachbuilding became the envy of the world. Luxurious interior fittings were matched by immaculate exterior bodywork. Although London coachbuilders were pre-eminent, many other cities and provincial towns had makers who turned out vehicles of the highest quality.

Abroad, it became the height of fashion to be driven by an English coachman in a London-built vehicle turned out with British harness, while at home, following royal leadership, noble and wealthy families maintained several types of carriage which were only seen as 'complete' if the horses, harness appointments and liveried servants complemented the turnout to the highest possible standard. Carriage exhibitions were held worldwide and the hope of royal patronage motivated every aspect of the trade.

For over a century the carriages ordered by successive sovereigns reflected the finest craftsmanship available over a wide range of vehicles. These ranged from closed state carriages and town coaches to the sporting and travelling open vehicles so popular in the Victorian and Edwardian fashionable worlds. Because all the carriages were made to order, each would vary slightly from the next, according to the coachbuilder's interpretation of his customer's personal requirements.

The last state carriage to be commissioned by a British ruler was in 1902, and by the reign of King George V motor cars had made their appearance in the Royal Mews.

In 1936 the accepted use of the motor car encouraged the new King, Edward VIII, to dispose of several of the lesser carriages that had been used in King George V's reign from the coach houses of London, Windsor, Sandringham and Balmoral. These were either presented to museums or, with their royal crests and cyphers removed, put up for private sale.

At the start of the Second World War, several owners of stately homes in the country offered to house the historic state coaches. However, with the exception of the Gold State Coach, which was stored under guard at Mentmore, the high cost and difficulty of transport meant that the Crown Equerry, Sir Dermot Kavanagh, used local storage at Windsor and Ascot.

In Scotland, fourteen carriages were put away in an iron shed at Abergeldie Castle and there they lay forgotten for the next twenty years. Some of them survived to become the stars of today's collection, because when King George VI (1936–52) agreed to further disposals after the

The 1902 State Landau

Queen Alexandra's State Coach

An Ascot Landau

The Bow-Fronted Clarence

A State Landau

The Ivory-Mounted Phaeton

war, out of sight was out of mind. At that time Sir Alexander Korda of London Film Productions bought nineteen royal carriages for a total sum of £1,700 for use as film props.

Over a hundred and five vehicles are still kept in the Royal Mews Buckingham Palace, Windsor Castle and Balmoral. Three-quarters of the collection is housed at either London or Windsor and all but a dozen are in working order.

The vehicles used today for official or ceremonial duties are either driven by a coachman from the box, or drawn by postilion-ridden horses, when they are termed posting or postilion vehicles. A postilion rides the near-side horse of a pair, and leads the off-side one. All vehicles for ceremonial carriage processions are directly approved by Her Majesty, and a combination of both coachman and postilion-driven vehicles may be chosen.

A hard-topped coach is referred to as a 'closed' coach, while landaus and other vehicles whose hoods can be broken open can be used as closed or open carriages. Except for the Ascot procession, an open carriage list will always include one or two approved hard-topped vehicles, referred to as 'wet weather carriages', so that last-minute changes can be made in case of bad weather.

In the past the carriages were always returned to their builders or other outside experts when they were in need of restoration. However, since 1982 they have been restored in the Mews. In addition, interior lighting, powered by concealed batteries, was finally installed in all the closed coaches for the Silver Jubilee of 1977.

Custom-built, each vehicle is treated as an individual by the Mews staff. To the coaching enthusiast, their histories are as much a part of their fascination as the pleasure in their continued use.

State vehicles have wheels and undercarriages painted in signal red, gilded and outlined in black. The wheels and undercarriages of other vehicles in the Royal Collection are royal claret and black lined in signal red.

Ivory fittings were a luxurious finish. This one is for a window pull to slide over, and shows the ivory knob for positioning the glass.

On a state coach, the frame of the coachman's seat is overlaid by an ornate cover known as a hammercloth. There are two theories about this name: either the cloth hid the tool box which contained a hammer, or else it was a useful place for concealing a provision hamper.

Hammercloths were made to the vehicle's measurements and followed the fashion of the moment. A separate costing for this cover was always specified in the initial estimate for a new coach. The firm of Tillett Racing Seats & Co Ltd are responsible for the Royal Mews hammercloths, which are still made to a traditional pattern.

The 1902 State Landau

Queen Alexandra's State Coach

An Ascot Landau

The Scottish State Coach

A Semi-State Landau

The Australian State Coach

Carriages have both shutters and windows, which work independently. Unlike the doors, these can be opened from either inside or outside.

One coach-building safety device is doors on state carriages that have no interior handles and require footmen to open the door from the outside. To do this in some cases it is necessary to lower the window and shutter, which reverses the two pins shown on the door shut.

As a point of etiquette, the hoods of landaus are not broken open until just before the passengers get in. Carriages leave the Mews with hoods and shutters closed. All brasswork is maintained by hand.

Sets of spikes were placed on the back of some coaches to stop street urchins jumping up for a free ride.

Hanging straps are essential for footmen to hold on to on the back of a vehicle. The Victorian bone-handled umbrella is a standard piece of carriage equipment.

The general and daily maintenance of the vehicles is carried out by the Head Carriage Restorer with his assistant and the carriage cleaners. Touching up paintwork on wheels marked by kerbs, and poles chewed by horses is commonplace, but keeping the body-work and undercarriages to the required standard is a skilled and time-consuming business.

8 The Irish State Coach

'. . . a state carriage built for me . . .'

Queen Victoria's Journal, 2 September 1853

John Hutton & Sons of Dublin were an established firm of coachbuilders who had held a Royal Warrant under King William IV and were re-appointed coachmakers to Queen Victoria in 1837. As a firm they were quick to point out that they had 'every facility for doing the work quickly and satisfactorily' and were at all times anxious to 'spare no exertion to show that Irish workmen are fully equal to do any work with which we might be entrusted'. Confident of the quality of their work, Hutton & Sons exhibited two of their carriages at the Great Exhibition staged in Hyde Park in 1851. It was after the exhibition that Hutton were invited by the Earl of Jersey, then Master of the Horse, to estimate for a new dress coach, 'made in the best-seasoned material and in the most perfect and highly finished style of workmanship'. The price Hutton quoted, which included the hammercloth, was £858.7.0, with a further £58.7.0 for the heraldic work.

Although this estimate was not accepted, Hutton went ahead and built a superb vehicle. A year later, with still no response from the Palace, they got permission to exhibit the carriage at the Great Industrial Exhibition held in Dublin in September 1853, where it was noticed and admired by both the Queen and Prince Albert. In October the initial estimate was suddenly accepted and the coach duly delivered to the Royal Mews nearly two years after the original approach.

After the death of the Prince Consort in 1861, the Queen refused to use the Gold State Coach, using the Irish-built carriage for the few state ceremonies she attended. On becoming Empress of India in 1876, she had an ornate gallery added to its roof.

After the Queen's death, King Edward VII found little use for the coach, and lent it to his eldest son, Prince George, who changed the existing heraldic work to that of the Heir Apparent.

Before his coronation as King George V in 1911, the coachbuilding firm of Barker & Co undertook to refurbish the vehicle in their Notting Hill workshops. It was here in early February that fire broke out and destroyed all the woodwork of the newly renovated coach; only the metal framework, made of finest English sword steel, and other pieces of ironwork were saved or left in any condition to use again. With less than nineteen weeks to go before the coronation date, Barker excelled themselves in reconstructing the coach from photographs and it was ready in time for the coronation procession, complete with its heraldic painting – a time-consuming undertaking in itself.

After the Second World War, with the Gold State Coach in need of repair, King George VI reverted to using the Irish State Coach for the Opening of Parliament and other ceremonial occasions, a custom followed by the present Queen. In 1960 Glover, Webb & Liversidge converted the coach so that when required it can be drawn by a team of postilion-ridden horses as well as coachman-driven from the box.

Opposite The spirit varnish used over the last seventy-seven years had caused great deterioration in the colour of the paint, and several layers had to be stripped off before it was discovered that the original colours of the vehicle were black and a dark shade of claret, instead of completely black as the restorers had previously assumed.

The brass casings of the four carriage lamps carry the rose, thistle and shamrock and appear in Hutton's original estimate.

The carved wooden supports and hind standards on either side of the footmen's cushion.

Apart from surface attention, little restoration had been done to the coach since 1911, and the New Year of 1988 found the vehicle in need of a complete repaint, overhaul and refurbishment. It was decided that, for the first time in the history of the Mews, the work should be done there by the resident Head Carriage Restorer, Mr Erik West, FRSA. His assistant was Martin Oates, a fourth-generation member of a Mews family, who had become on leaving school the first member of staff to do a five-year indentured apprenticeship in carriage restoration. This had been undertaken and completed in the Mews under West's supervision.

The project, which was fitted around the general routine of the Paint Shop, took nearly eighteen months to complete and cost the carriage restorers many sleepless nights. The old traditions of quality in coach-building were upheld throughout, with West co-ordinating the outside tradesmen, all of whom held Royal Warrants of Appointment. During the restoration many questions on the coach's previous history were answered.

After successful trials, the Irish State Coach was once more seen in public, when, put to a team of Windsor Greys driven from the box, Her Majesty travelled to Westminster for the State Opening of Parliament in November 1989.

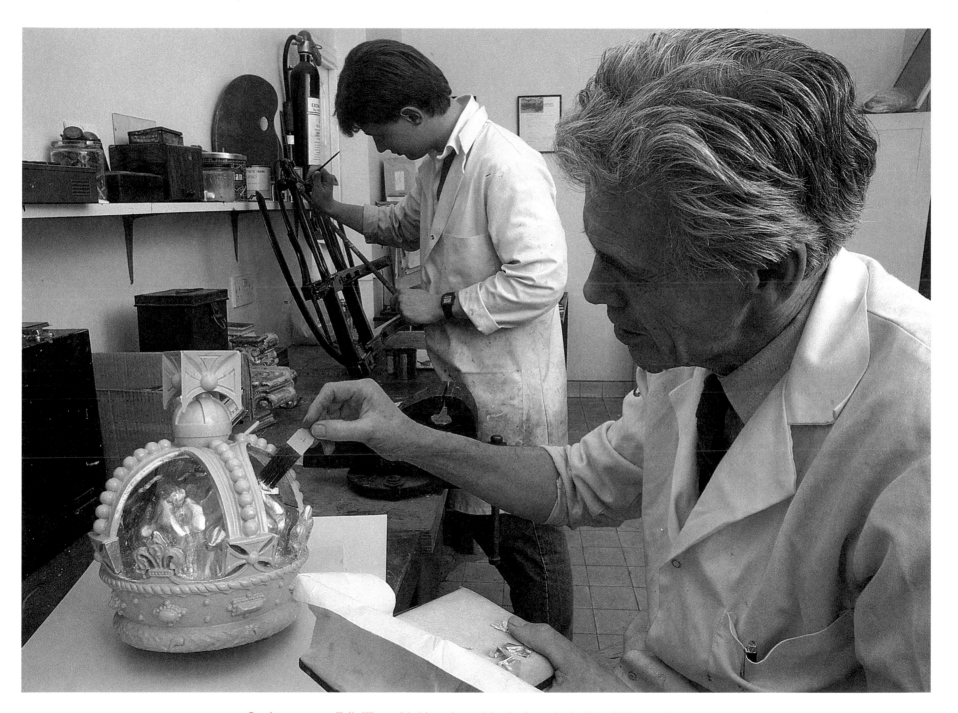

Carriage restorer Erik West with his assistant Martin Oates in the Royal Mews Paint Shop.

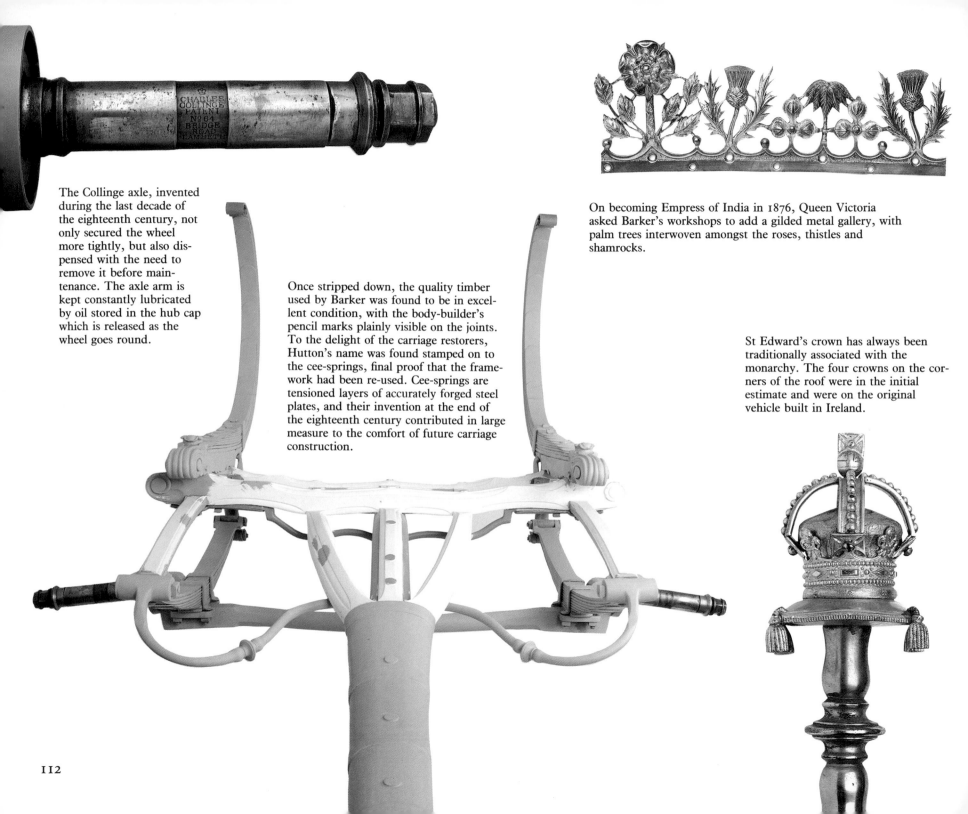

The Collinge axle, invented during the last decade of the eighteenth century, not only secured the wheel more tightly, but also dispensed with the need to remove it before maintenance. The axle arm is kept constantly lubricated by oil stored in the hub cap which is released as the wheel goes round.

Once stripped down, the quality timber used by Barker was found to be in excellent condition, with the body-builder's pencil marks plainly visible on the joints. To the delight of the carriage restorers, Hutton's name was found stamped on to the cee-springs, final proof that the framework had been re-used. Cee-springs are tensioned layers of accurately forged steel plates, and their invention at the end of the eighteenth century contributed in large measure to the comfort of future carriage construction.

On becoming Empress of India in 1876, Queen Victoria asked Barker's workshops to add a gilded metal gallery, with palm trees interwoven amongst the roses, thistles and shamrocks.

St Edward's crown has always been traditionally associated with the monarchy. The four crowns on the corners of the roof were in the initial estimate and were on the original vehicle built in Ireland.

112

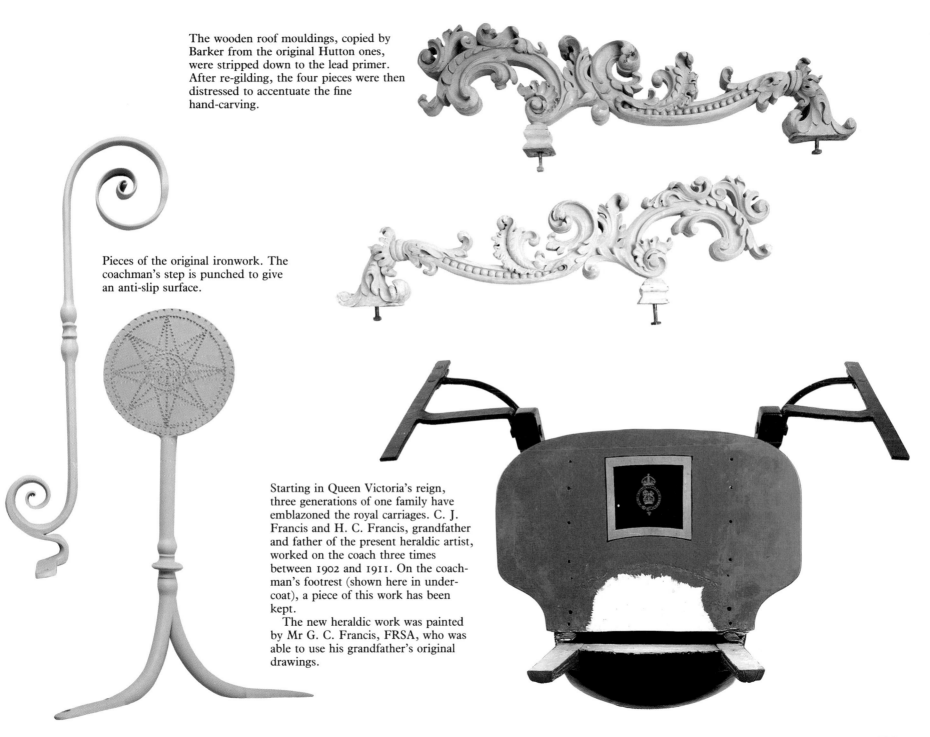

The wooden roof mouldings, copied by Barker from the original Hutton ones, were stripped down to the lead primer. After re-gilding, the four pieces were then distressed to accentuate the fine hand-carving.

Pieces of the original ironwork. The coachman's step is punched to give an anti-slip surface.

Starting in Queen Victoria's reign, three generations of one family have emblazoned the royal carriages. C. J. Francis and H. C. Francis, grandfather and father of the present heraldic artist, worked on the coach three times between 1902 and 1911. On the coachman's footrest (shown here in undercoat), a piece of this work has been kept.

The new heraldic work was painted by Mr G. C. Francis, FRSA, who was able to use his grandfather's original drawings.

Above Under the roof lining, it was found that Barker had strengthened the mahogany timbers in the traditional way of coachbuilders, using glued off-cuts to hold the shape.

Opposite Twenty metres of silk damask were used on the sunburst ceiling. The rose in the centre hides the bolt which secures the crown and cushion to the outside of the roof.

24-carat English loose-leaf gold was double-gilded to the wooden hand-carved central crown.

Before the final two coats of varnish, the Head Carriage Restorer finished the filigree work with three shades of umber and sienna oil-based glaze.

The Royal Electrical and Mechanical Engineers provided both ingenuity and machinery to separate and rejoin the undercarriage and the body.

The widely dished wheels and cranked axles of the vehicle give extra strength and allow the body to be slung lower on the undercarriage. Here the new cee-spring leathers, one inch thick at the widest part, start to take the body weight.

All the leatherwork was renewed and stitched by hand in the workshops of Keith Luxford, harness maker to the Queen.

Twenty coats of colour were applied by brush to the entire coach. The linseed Alkyd-type paint matched to the original colour was supplied by Joseph Mason of Derby, master paintmakers since 1800.

9 Queen Alexandra's State Coach

'The Crown is, according to the saying,
"the Fountain of Honour".'

Walter Bagehot 1826–77

Apart from the coronation ceremony, the Imperial State Crown is only worn by the sovereign at the State Opening of Parliament.

Formerly, the Regalia was brought by the Royal Watermen upriver from the Tower of London directly to the Palace of Westminster. Today, however, the Crown and Regalia travel earlier by road under police escort to Buckingham Palace.

On the morning of the ceremony, the Crown, together with the Sword of State and Cap of Maintenance, is taken from Buckingham Palace to the Palace of Westminster by Gentlemen of the Household travelling in horse-drawn carriages with a Regalia escort of the Household Cavalry. The Queen's Bargemaster and Royal Watermen retain a place in the procession and travel on the backs of the carriages.

The carriage in which the Imperial State Crown travels is Queen Alexandra's State Coach. Originally a closed town coach, it was altered by Hooper in 1893. With the addition of chamfered glass windows, the coach was often used by Their Royal Highnesses the Prince and Princess of Wales (later King Edward VII and Queen Alexandra) to attend official and private engagements away from their home at Marlborough House. After the death of King Edward VII, Queen Alexandra continued to use the coach for a time but later returned it to the Royal Mews.

Of all the state coaches, 'the Alix' has a special charm. The unusual domed roof and curved doors are complemented by the curved undercarriage and a profusion of heraldic decoration that sports no less than sixty-seven crowns. The Imperial State Crown rests on a removable table lit with special lights inside the carriage, so that on the route to Westminster the symbol of sovereignty is clearly visible.

Above The Crown procession leaves the Grand Entrance, Buckingham Palace, for the Palace of Westminster.

Opposite The present Imperial State Crown was designed and made for Queen Victoria in 1837 and weighs 21 lbs 13 oz.

For the coronation of Queen Elizabeth II in 1953 the shape of the arches was altered to reduce the height. It is set with over 2,800 diamonds, and the history of many of the larger stones is of as much interest as their value.

In the traditional cross, mounted on a globe to signify Christ's dominance over the world, the sapphire is reputed to have come from the ring of Edward the Confessor.

A red stone was always considered lucky, and the semi-precious spinel known as the Black Prince's Ruby was returned to King Charles II by a well-wisher who bought it for £4 after the Crown Jewels were sold during the years of Cromwell's Protectorate.

The centre diamond is still the second largest diamond in the world. It is a part of the Cullinan Stone, mined in 1905, and is referred to as the Second Star of Africa.

Gold-tooled leatherwork underneath the bottom carriage step is only seen when the steps are raised. The leatherwork rests against the closed door.

The interior of the coach is upholstered in blue damask. All the state coaches have door pockets.

Above The wheels and undercarriage are hand-painted.

Opposite Heraldry is a system of instant recognition. Although it has become a stylized art form, their individual style on the devices they paint marks the work of heraldic artists as essentially their own.

Repainting the bodywork of a vehicle does not necessarily mean the removal of the heraldic work; the body colour can be painted round it and the whole panel subsequently revarnished. The coat of arms was painted by Mr C. J. Francis, the grandfather of The Queen's present heraldic artist.

10 King Edward VII's Town Coach

'We were very silent in the carriage;
it swayed gently and creaked a little
like a small boat at sea.'

From *Clementine Churchill*
by her daughter Mary Soames, 1979

The Town Coach was ordered by King Edward VII from the coachbuilding firm of Hooper, but it was not finished until after his death in 1910.

It was one of seventeen similar coaches in the Royal Mews that would have been painted in the royal livery colours with a discreet royal cypher on the door. Used with a dark blue hammercloth over the coachman's box and drawn by a pair of bay horses, these dignified closed vehicles were used to convey distinguished visitors to and from Buckingham Palace very much as royal cars are used now.

After the Second World War, all the town coaches were disposed of with the exception of the one used today, which was stored at Windsor Castle. Restored in 1963, extra glass windows were added, making it more suitable for modern use.

The inside of the carriage is upholstered in leather and bears a silver plaque commemorating its part in the state funeral procession of Sir Winston Churchill in 1965, when Lady Churchill and her two daughters travelled in it behind the gun carriage bearing the statesman's coffin.

One of the coach's most impressive duties each year is to carry to the State Opening of Parliament the two Serjeants-at-Arms on duty who act as escorts to the Crown. The Serjeants-at-Arms place the heads of their maces through the windows of the coach to show their symbolic authority and protection of the Crown.

With three Royal Watermen on the back, King Edward VII's Town Coach travels second in the Crown procession that leaves Buckingham Palace twenty-three minutes ahead of The Queen.

THIS COACH WAS USED TO CONVEY LADY CHURCHILL
FROM WESTMINSTER HALL TO ST. PAULS CATHEDRAL
AND ON TO TOWER PIER,
ON THE OCCASION OF THE STATE FUNERAL OF
SIR WINSTON CHURCHILL, K.G., O.M., C.H.
ON 30TH. JANUARY 1965.

IT WAS DRIVEN BY THE HEAD COACHMAN MR. J. COOZE,
DRAWN BY TWO DUTCH BAY HORSES
'CAPETOWN' AND 'BLOEMFONTEIN' BOTH AGED 22 YEARS.

At the State Opening of Parliament, the Town Coach carries the two Serjeants-at-Arms on duty and their maces to the Palace of Westminster.

Serjeants-at-Arms make up one of the oldest bodyguards in existence, and their formation is believed to date from the reign of King Richard I. Later, as a band of knights or gentlemen of high degree, they were responsible for the sovereign's personal protection and invested with authority to execute his commands.

Their maces, made of silver gilt, are extremely heavy to carry and are two of ten kept in the Tower of London. Originally a short-handled weapon heavy enough to beat in an opponent's steel helmet, they have developed into ceremonial staffs and are symbolic of authority and protection.

11 State and Semi-State Landaus

'The six dress landaus are what H.M. alludes to.
They open very badly, but still they do open
and have been used that way recently.'

Letter from Colonel Maude to Sir Henry Ponsonby,
5 January 1887

Landaus can be drawn by postilion-ridden or coachman-driven horses and were very popular in the mid-nineteenth century, when their design was perfected. Their chief asset was the way in which the double hoods could be broken open, making the vehicles suitable for both town and country use in all weather conditions.

Dress landaus were used on important occasions by royalty and members of the nobility. They were ornamented with armorial bearings and the boxes covered with ornate hammercloths. In town two well-matched horses were driven by a coachman in state livery with two footmen up behind.

Road landaus were used for travelling. Privately owned, they were an impressive turnout drawn by a team of postilion-ridden horses and attended by two liveried outriders mounted on horses that matched the team. However, after the arrival of the railways, both types of royal vehicle were only used for short distances and park outings.

Queen Victoria enjoyed being driven behind a postilion-ridden team, and by the year of her Golden Jubilee in 1887 had adopted the habit of using a plain road landau for both public and private events. The Queen's refusal to abandon her widow's weeds for the 'full dress' which would have been in keeping with the Gold State Coach, meant that plans for her Golden Jubilee procession caused the greatest anxiety to her Crown Equerry, Colonel Maude.

Faced with the difficulty of producing an open carriage procession of appropriate grandeur, Maude reluctantly agreed to refurbishing six dress landaus and, with very bad grace, to decorating and gilding the road landaus. In a letter to the Queen's private secretary, Sir Henry Ponsonby, he pointed out that 'there are two Scotch servants up behind and their dress does not harmonise with a great deal of gilding'. Only weeks away from the celebrations, he mentioned to Ponsonby that he was 'anxious about leaving The Queen in London without a plain road landau. Do you think she understands that she will have to use these painted up and gilded landaus . . . for this season at all events?'

Evidently Her Majesty was delighted at the transformation of her carriages, and for both her Golden and Diamond Jubilee processions elected to use what she described in her diary as 'a handsome gilt landau' drawn by postilion-ridden horses.

Of the several well decorated landaus still in use today, the dress landaus are termed State Landaus, and the road vehicles Semi-State Landaus. They are constantly used for official and ceremonial duties, and both types of vehicle are seen in London on the many days throughout the year when Her Majesty receives newly appointed ambassadors and High Commissioners at Buckingham Palace.

Accompanied by a member of Her Majesty's Household, the Marshal of the Diplomatic Corps, ambassadors travel in a State Landau coachman-driven to a pair, while High Commissioners are accorded the privilege of a Semi-State Landau drawn by two postilion-ridden pairs.

Opposite   His Majesty King George V with Queen Mary and Princess Mary inspect the State and Semi-State Landaus in the Mews on 30 May 1912.

Of the eight State Landaus still in use today, the first one was built in 1838, the year of Queen Victoria's coronation. Additional ones were acquired at various dates until 1872.

Five Semi-State Landaus are still in use.

State or dress landaus were similar in appointment and design to closed dress carriages. However, the difficulty of perfecting watertight hoods that would lie flat when they were opened added a considerable amount of money to the initial estimate for a dress coach.

The correctly tinctured quarters of the Royal Arms are indicated on the brass head plates by different dots and lines.

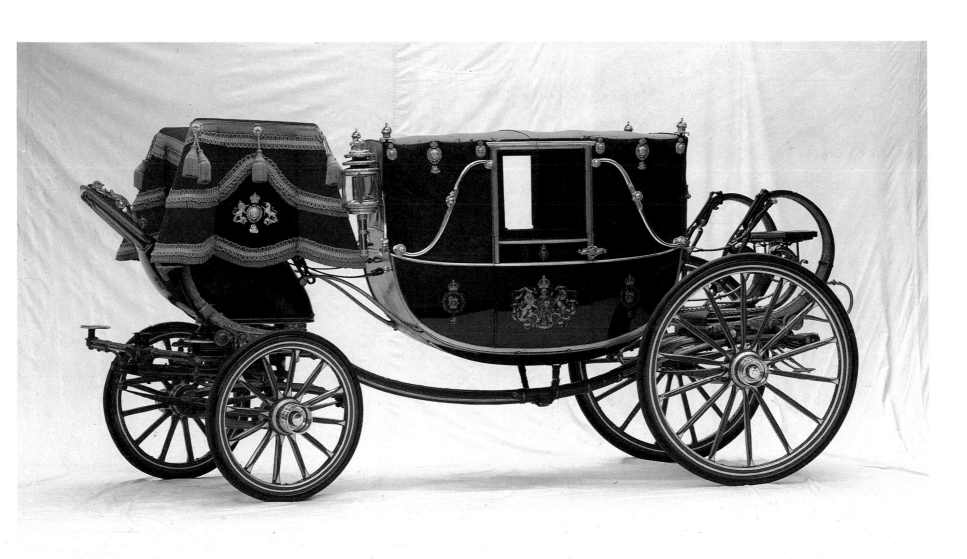

A State Landau.

Above Each carriage lamp has its own original canvas-covered spring which gradually raises the candle to the right height as it burns down.

Opposite Very few carriage doors can be opened from the inside, and the carriage steps must be put up before the door can be closed.On cold mornings, brass hot water bottles are filled before the carriages leave the Mews.

Above The undercarriages of the State Landaus are quite heavily carved. Each vehicle has its own pole with a corresponding number on the pole hole. The pole is held in place by the pole pin, and it is impossible to swap poles, for each landau has a different size and fitting. A pole acts as the tiller to the carriage.

Opposite State Landaus leave the Grand Entrance, Buckingham Palace, for the State Opening of Parliament.

The Semi-State Landaus were not decorated and gilded until Queen Victoria's Golden Jubilee in 1887.

A Semi-State Landau. The vehicles all have a brake, worked from the footmen's seat, for which the senior man is responsible.

The Prince of Wales accompanied by Prince Andrew drives in the 1902 State Landau to his wedding in July 1981.

12 The 1902 State Landau

'It is undoubtedly the handsomest
equipage in the country.'

The Times, 19 June 1902

On his accession in January 1901, the new King Edward VII was already fifty-nine years old. Possessed of both charm and style, he combined diplomacy with a natural flair for showmanship, and after sixty-four years of Victorian formality, colour and flamboyance were to be the hallmarks of the new reign.

The King wanted a splendid new open carriage in which to drive through the streets of London on the second day of his coronation festivities. Although the road landaus had been gilded, unlike his mother he did not feel that they were in keeping with the impressive moroccan state harness and the cream stallions that he wanted to use.

Following the late Queen's custom of using a postilion landau for state ceremonial occasions, it was decided that the new vehicle should follow the same design but be on a larger and more impressive scale.

The Landau was built in the Chelsea workshops of Hooper & Co., coachbuilders to the King. Its manufacture was entirely British and it was mostly made of British materials. It was also fitted with such contemporary innovations as india-rubber tyres. Without a coachman's seat, the generous splasher or mudguard curving over the fore-carriage was a notable feature, and it was covered in crimson leather, as opposed to the usual black, in order to tone in with the red moroccan harness.

The upholstery was in the same material and colour as the newly refurbished interior of the Gold State Coach, and the bodywork painted in a lighter shade of purple lake than that used on the other landaus.

Forty-eight hours before the coronation day, which was fixed for 26 June 1902, the country was dismayed to hear that the King was to be operated on for acute appendicitis. The ceremony was therefore postponed until August and, bearing in mind that the King would still be convalescent then, the second day's festivities were cancelled. It was not until 21 October 1902 that the King was able to use his new landau, when for the first time he drove in state to the City of London.

Since its first appearance 'the 1902' has been part of countless royal pageants and it was the carriage in which both the present Prince of Wales and the Duke of York returned to Buckingham Palace with their brides after their wedding ceremonies.

Both the interior and exterior have been kept in the original colours. One distinctive feature is the pattern of acorns and oak leaves found throughout the vehicle. Carved and gilded bands of this device are used around the body.

Weather permitting, the Landau is always used as the number one carriage in which Her Majesty accompanies foreign heads of state on the ceremonial drive after their arrival in this country.

Put to a team of six grey horses, the 1902 is taken over the processional route during the early-morning rehearsal before a state visit. Exercise brakes and other carriages form the rest of the rehearsal procession.

Postilion carriages are used for both days of a state visit.

The gilt buckles on the sway straps, the carriage lamps and the crowns on the folding leather hoods were especially made for the Landau in London workshops.

For early-morning rehearsals in winter carriage lamps are lit.
All the metalwork shows the acorn and oak-leaf device used throughout the 1902.

The brass pole head of the 1902 is the only one amongst the Carriage Collection embossed with a crown.

Only seen by the footmen, the underneath of the folding carriage steps matches the rest of the red moroccan leatherwork.

Royal footmen in attendance are taught to place a foot on the bottom step of any carriage to help keep the vehicle steady as the passengers enter and alight.

147

Above A final touch of hoof oil for the grey team, and the 1902 State Landau is ready to leave the Mews quadrangle for the start of a summer state visit.

Opposite 0600 hours at Victoria Station on a rehearsal morning.

To stop the carriage rocking forward as Her Majesty mounts the steps, the liveried chockman places two chocking sticks on either side of the off-side back wheel. Once the procession is ready to start, skill has to be exercised to remove the front chock quickly enough before the carriage jolts over it.

13 The Scottish State Coach

'I have unearthed the full story of the Semi State Road
Landau, about which we corresponded last year.'

Letter to Brigadier Sir Walter Sale (Crown Equerry 1955–61)
from the ninth Earl of Albemarle,
14 September 1959

During the early part of the nineteenth century it was common practice for members of the Royal Family to vie with each other in the luxury, elegance and individuality of the carriages their coach builders made for them. Adams & Hooper of the Haymarket were particularly well known for the excellence of their travelling carriages, and it was therefore a challenge to the firm's skill when the Duke of Cambridge, a younger brother of William IV, invited them in 1830 to build him a state coach for the new King's coronation procession.

The commissioned coach was so admired that the firm soon established a reputation as builders of state vehicles, while this coach remains the basis of what, over a hundred and thirty years later, came to be known as the Scottish State Coach.

It was used as an enclosed town coach by the Cambridge family for many years until it was sold to the eighth Earl of Albemarle. After using it at the coronation of King Edward VII in 1902, the Earl later had it converted to an open postilion road landau, which he lent to the King during His Majesty's state visit to Norwich just before he died in 1910.

In June 1920, Lord Albemarle – by now a Lord in Waiting to King George V – presented the carriage to Queen Mary. The Queen found little use for it, and it was stored in the mews at Windsor Castle. Here, referred to as the Cambridge Coach, it fell into disrepair.

In the mid 1960s great interest was aroused by the news that The Queen would attend in person the General Assembly of Ministers and Elders of the Church of Scotland in Edinburgh, the first time that a reigning sovereign had attended such a ceremony since the union of the two crowns in 1603. It was decided that, to honour this unique occasion, The Queen would travel in a state carriage from the Palace of Holyrood to Saint Giles's Cathedral. From here the idea developed that the Cambridge Coach should be refurbished and named the Scottish State Coach.

The major part of the work, therefore, was carried out by St Cuthbert's Co-operative Society in Edinburgh from drawings supplied by Glover, Webb & Liversidge of London. The coach was given a completely new top, with large glass windows. Two transparent panels in the roof give added light and provide an excellent view of the interior for people looking down from above.

From the Crown of Scotland, which is kept in Edinburgh Castle, a fibre-glass model was made by the London Co-operative Society to place on the top of the coach. After consultation with Scotland's senior herald, the Lord Lyon King of Arms, The Queen approved the Royal Arms of Scotland emblazoned upon the doors of the coach and the insignia of the Most Ancient and Most Noble Order of the Thistle on the quarter panels. The pattern of the brass gallery around the roof was taken from the one on the light fitting that hangs between the King's Door and the Equerries' Room in Buckingham Palace.

Opposite Referred to in the Mews as 'the Scottish', this coach is not restricted to use in Scotland. The ease with which the occupants can be seen makes it an elegant and practical vehicle for days when doubtful weather means that an open carriage cannot be used.

Above King James VI of Scotland came to the English throne as James I in 1603. As the first Stuart king, he banished the red Tudor dragon from the sinister side of the Royal Coat of Arms in favour of a Scottish unicorn, since when the lion and unicorn have been used as the English royal supporters. On the Royal Arms for use in Scotland, however, the unicorn is seen as the dexter supporter. The quarter panel bears the insignia of the Most Ancient and Most Noble Order of the Thistle, established by King James II in 1687 as the premier order of chivalry in Scotland. The collar is decorated with devices of thistles and sprigs of rue, symbolising Picts and Scots.

Opposite Transparent panels in the roof of the coach add extra light. The carriage is often used on the second day of a state visit to take a visiting head of state from Buckingham Palace to St James's Palace. Here he receives the High Commissioners for the Commonwealth countries and ambassadors accredited to the Court of St James's.

14 The Ivory-Mounted Phaeton

'After The Queen had decided to use a carriage
for her Birthday Parade,
I had about five different ones brought out
and Her Majesty chose this one.'

Lieutenant Colonel Sir John Miller (Crown Equerry 1961–87)
to the author

It was Phaeton, son of the sun god Helios, who scorched the rim of Earth when, going against his father's wishes, he drove and lost control of the fiery team put to the god's chariot.

The main character of this myth of Ancient Greece gave his name to the original design of all owner-driven, four-wheel carriages fitted with forward-facing seats. Driven by the Prince Regent and his dandified contemporaries, these fast late-eighteenth-century vehicles put to a team or a pair became the forerunners of the modern sports car. Partly superseded in the early nineteenth century by the even more hair-raising two-wheeled curricle, phaetons continued to be made, incorporating many different names and designs. By 1824 the increasing girth of King George IV started a fashion for low-slung vehicles which were convenient to get in and out of. Later, owing to the ease with which they accommodated the crinoline, elegant variations of the same carriage put to a single horse or a pair became popular as park or ladies' phaetons. These were much favoured in the summer months by ladies who, with or without a companion, found them charming vehicles for the obligatory social pastime of 'taking an airing'.

Although The Queen had only used it occasionally before 1987, the Ivory-Mounted Phaeton has since then become one of the best-known carriages in the Royal Collection. It was built for Queen Victoria in 1842 by Barker & Co. at an estimated cost of £300: the specifications state that it was 'to be painted and lined in the royal colours' and have 'ivory ornaments'. These latter are unique and take the place of fittings which would otherwise have been made in brass.

The Phaeton was one of the first cee-spring pair-horsed carriages to be made. However, in keeping with Victorian prudery, the mudguard or splasher, made to hide the horses' hindquarters from the passengers' sight, was built so high that it is doubtful that the vehicle could ever have been passenger-driven. Contemporary pictures show that it was drawn by two or four postilion-ridden horses and that is how the public see it used today.

The Queen's Official Birthday Parade in June has become a national event, and with world-wide television coverage it reaches an audience of millions. When in 1986 Her Majesty decided to retire her twenty-four-year-old Canadian police charger, Burmese, that she had ridden in the Parade for eighteen consecutive years, there was general disappointment. It was later announced that Her Majesty would attend the ceremony in a carriage, but as to which carriage both press and public could only speculate.

The Queen's decision to substitute the Phaeton for a horse in her procession instead of one of her more imposing carriages is entirely practical. Drawn by a postilion-ridden pair, it is easy to manoeuvre during the inspection, and, travelling with the steps already let down and without doors to open, time is saved when Her Majesty gets in and out at the saluting dais.

Once the choice of vehicle had been made, the Phaeton went into the Royal Mews Paint Shop to undergo restoration. Not having been in regular use, the wheels had completely dried out and collapsed beyond repair. They were replaced and re-tyred by Crofords of Ashford around

Opposite Her Majesty returning at the head of her guards after the Birthday Parade. The Crown Equerry rides on the right of the picture.

the existing Collinge axles. All the paintwork was restored to show condition, and canework re-applied to a split panel. The ivory was re-polished and where pieces were missing new ones stained to match the existing colour. The Buckingham Palace upholsterers redesigned the back of the seat to make it more comfortable for Her Majesty to sit forward. Because of the unusual length of the cee-springs in comparison to the length of the carriage, extra sway straps were used to fix the body firmly down on the chassis and eliminate any unnecessary movement.

From the end of May the two horses chosen to draw the Phaeton are put to an exercise vehicle and worked as a postilion-ridden pair. On leaving the Palace, the Phaeton is kept at a fair walking pace; with fit horses this can be difficult to maintain, and it is important that the pair chosen is well ridden in and aware of exactly what is required of them.

In preparation for the Birthday Parade, two 'reviews' are held. In the Royal Mews the detail of them both is much the same as for the main event. The exceptions are in the various harness appointments and the liveries used. Plain livery is worn for the first review taken by the Major General, Semi-State for the second, or the Colonel's review, and Full State for the occasion itself. On the Phaeton harness the badges of the Guards regiment trooping the colour are screwed onto the blinkers and centre drops of the horses' bridles; on the day, blue regimental fronts, or brow bands, and rosettes are added, and the correct ceremonial state saddle cloths are worn under the harness.

The first news of the use of these saddle cloths in 1987 caused the then Lieutenant Colonel commanding Scots Guards to send a cryptic message to the Crown Equerry, saying he had heard a rumour that there was a Scots Guards state saddle cloth being cut up and that he hoped it wasn't true. The Crown Equerry replied that he was indeed cutting up a Scots Guards state saddle cloth but that it was at the express wish of the regiment's Colonel in Chief, whose property it was!

As Colonel in Chief of the five footguard regiments, Her Majesty owns five traditional state saddle cloths, embroidered with the appropriate regimental insignia on each side. With two horses now involved, the Crown Equerry had, with Her Majesty's approval, had the original cloths made into pairs by cutting them down the centre and replacing the inner sides, which are unseen by the public, with plain material.

The two consecutive Saturday reviews and the Saturday of the Birthday Parade itself are kept to a tight timetable in the Mews. Reviews cancelled because of bad weather are put back to the afternoon and if the entire day is ruled out, the Sunday can be used. Morning stables start at 5.30 a.m. and all horses have one good hour of exercise either in or out of the school before each parade.

The empty Phaeton proceeds exactly as if Her Majesty were present on both reviews, going to and from the Buckingham Palace quadrangle by way of the Coachman's Gate at the rear of the Mews and through the Palace garden.

As well as turning out two barouches for the Queen Mother, the Mews is also responsible for the chargers of the Royal Colonels, the Master of the Horse, the Crown Equerry and the appointments of the horses of the mounted equerries for all three parades.

On the day of the procession the 'tack vehicle' (a horse-drawn covered brake) is loaded with grooming kit, spare harness, best rugs, mackintoshes, chocks and mounting blocks and goes ahead to Horse Guards. A minibus will take the chockmen and horse-holders, with the sergeant farrier and harness maker in attendance with their bags of tools in case of emergencies.

Opposite Head Coachman, Arthur Showell, wearing plain postilion livery, takes the Ivory-Mounted Phaeton through the gardens of Buckingham Palace on the way to the King's Door in the quadrangle for the first review.

15 The Barouches

Barouche: (ba-roosh)

New English Dictionary

Barouches were luxurious open carriages used throughout the nineteenth century and were popular with society as summertime park or town vehicles. They were expensive to maintain since fashion dictated that a barouche should have horses of a superior quality to those used for other carriages.

The Dowager Queen Adelaide, wife of King William IV, gave a miniature barouche as a Christmas present to Queen Victoria's children in 1846, and this delightful little carriage is still in the Royal Collection. In her journal Queen Victoria recorded that on receiving the gift, 'the five children were in the greatest delight' and, although the carriage can be drawn by either a donkey or a pony, it was the gentlemen in attendance who were immediately 'put to' in King George IV's long corridor at Windsor Castle.

Until the introduction of motor cars and their admission to Hyde Park, an essential ingredient of the summer season was the fashionable morning or evening hour spent riding or driving in the park. Horseflesh, carriages and tailors' and dressmakers' skills were all under intense scrutiny, and high prices were paid to obtain the desired perfection. The highlight of any evening parade was the arrival of Her Royal Highness the Princess of Wales in a 'splendidly turned out barouche' when, according to the Duke of Portland, it was 'usual for all other carriages to remain as far as possible at a standstill'.

There are two of these distinctive carriages in the Royal Collection, both made by Barker, who were then based in Chandos Street. Coachman-driven to a pair of horses, they are used during the summer months and always carry the Queen Mother, her guests and members of her household to and from Horse Guards Parade for the Queen's Birthday Parade.

The carriages themselves resemble old-fashioned perambulators, and, in fine weather with the apron folded back, can seat up to four passengers. Their high suspension and construction are responsible for a strong rocking movement which, even with assistance, makes the downward-slanting passenger steps difficult to negotiate with dignity.

Both barouches were in constant use during the ninetieth birthday celebrations of Her Majesty Queen Elizabeth the Queen Mother in the summer of 1990.

Detail from a photograph of Queen Mary and Princess Mary with the Prince of Wales and Prince George, driving in a barouche to the King's Birthday Parade, 29 May 1911.

Queen Elizabeth the Queen Mother and the Princess of Wales with Prince William and Prince Harry returning to Buckingham Palace in a barouche after the Queen's Birthday Parade, 16 June 1990.

16 Five Ascot Landaus

'The carriages were Landaus and all open . . .
each with four horses,
the postilions in their State Ascot jackets and caps.'

Queen Victoria's Journal, 12 June 1838

The week of the Royal Ascot race meeting finds the relevant carriages, horses, harness and livery installed in the mews at Windsor Castle. The five open postilion carriages with painted basketwork sides that are used throughout the week are known as the Ascot Landaus and they are well over a hundred years old. Various coachbuilders constructed these light vehicles for Queen Victoria and they have since been used on many different occasions.

Queen Anne was the first monarch to drive in procession from Windsor to Ascot, where in August 1711 she opened the inaugural race meeting. Subsequently, King George IV established the custom of driving up the course, as the diarist Thomas Creevy put it, 'in the presence of everybody'.

Internationally famous for its unique blend of royal patronage, racing and fashion, the four-day meeting is one of the summer's most important social events. Unless racing is abandoned because of the weather, the daily carriage procession of Her Majesty provides an unforgettable setting in which to see The Queen and members of her family.

The carriage distance through Windsor Home Park to the racecourse is roughly six miles. Attended by a motorized tack vehicle, the procession leaves the mews shortly after mid-day, with plenty of time to settle the horses, check the harness, deal with any emergency, and, weather permitting, break open the hoods, before arriving at Duke's Lane to wait for The Queen.

It is here, in the heart of the park, surrounded by officials and the public, that the royal party exchange their motor cars for the carriages. Once on the racecourse, the procession opens out to achieve the correct spacing. An outrider must be seen to lead his carriage forward and not seem to be attached to the one in front.

After Her Majesty's arrival at the Royal Enclosure, the empty carriages are taken over the road to a covered way. Here there is a short rest before the Ascots are driven home across the park. The Queen and her guests later return to the castle by car.

On the return of the Landaus to the mews, preparations are immediately put in hand for the following day's procession. 'The whole thing,' as Creevy noted in 1825, will look 'very splendid; in short, quite as it should be'.

Opposite The Queen and the Duke of Edinburgh, accompanied by the Prince of Wales and the Master of the Horse, the Earl of Westmorland enter the grandstand enclosure on Ascot racecourse in an Ascot Landau.

The procession and service of the Order of the Garter at Windsor is held on the Monday of Ascot Week every year. If the weather is fine, three Ascot Landaus are used to return Her Majesty and members of her family from the steps of St George's Chapel up the hill to the Sovereign's Entrance in the castle quadrangle.

Above The buildings and stables which form the mews at Windsor were erected by Queen Victoria in 1842 and represent much of her contribution to the castle's nineteenth-century reconstruction.

Over page The carriage procession pauses in the Home Park. The Landau hoods are broken open and a final inspection is made before approaching Duke's Lane.

When any carriage procession is at a standstill, the leading outriders turn to face the front vehicles. Turning again to face the direction of travel warns those involved with carriages and horses that the procession is about to move off. The leading outriders show the way and indicate the paying of compliments.

Above There can be no lingering between motor and horse-drawn vehicles, for a late arrival by the carriage procession past the stands holds up jockeys crossing from the weighing room to the paddock for the first race.

Opposite Postilions, outriders and mews staff relax after the six-mile drive from Windsor Castle.

The Lady Diana Spencer is seen through the windows of the Glass Coach as she is driven to her wedding in St Paul's Cathedral on 29 July 1981.

17 The Glass Coach

'Nothing ever becomes real till it is experienced . . .'

John Keats, 1795–1821

Each year, visitors to the main coach house in the Mews pause before an elegant carriage, less ornate than a state coach but obviously a vehicle of quality. The printed notice beside it explains that the Princess Royal, the Princess of Wales and the Duchess of York all drove in it to their weddings. The list fleetingly evokes daydreams of princes, slippers and pumpkins, before returning the visitor to reality, and the knowledge that very few people ever drive in a royal carriage.

The Glass Coach in the Royal Mews is often referred to as the wedding or bridal coach. It was built in 1881 by the firm of John W. Peters & Sons for the use of Sir John Whitaker Ellis, Lord Mayor of London Elect. As a personal friend of Ellis, the coachbuilder took immense pains with the design and construction of the carriage, and insisted on being carried from his deathbed to view the finished vehicle. Used as a town coach by subsequent lord mayors, it remained the property of Peters & Sons until 1911.

Only weeks before the coronation of King George V, fire destroyed a royal coach that was to be used in the procession, and this misfortune enabled A. J. Peters to offer his father's glass coach for sale to the Crown. According to a statement from Mr Peters in the Mews archives, the firm was proud to turn the vehicle out in state in record time, since when it has played an increasingly romantic part at the weddings of the immediate Royal Family.

Traditional snakes' heads terminate the shackles which are attached by leather straps and large brass buckles to the cee-spring leathers. Those made for the Glass Coach are the finest in the entire Carriage Collection.

The term 'glass coach' refers to any coach whose upper panels are made of glass instead of being filled with wood or leather.

When repairing the heraldic work on the quarter panels in 1978, Mr G. C. Francis used his grandfather's and father's original drawings.

The panels are painted with the collar of the Most Noble Order of the Garter, from which is suspended the Great George. The order was founded by Edward III in the fourteenth century and is the premier order of chivalry of Great Britain.

Lamps on late-nineteenth-century coaches used candles to provide the light.

It is correct coaching procedure always to show that the wick on a new candle has been previously lit and is therefore usable.

Miss Sarah Ferguson travels for the first time in a closed royal carriage as the Glass Coach carries her to her wedding with the Duke of York in Westminster Abbey on 23 July 1986.

18 The Balmoral Sociable

'My own dear Scotch sociable was at the station . . .'

Queen Victoria's Journal, August 1868

Attended by members of her household, Queen Victoria arrived at Lucerne station on 7 August 1868, accompanied by her two youngest daughters, the twenty- and eleven-year-old Princesses Louise and Beatrice. Her pleasure at finding one of her favourite carriages waiting to meet her in these unfamiliar surroundings was an auspicious beginning to a rare informal holiday. Joined later by the sixteen-year-old haemophilic Prince Leopold, the Queen and her children spent the next four weeks combining pleasure and education in trips and excursions into the surrounding countryside and mountains.

In spite of the presence of local guides, and coachmen driving teams of small, sure-footed horses, these expeditions were not without their hazards.

Even the Queen, whose enthusiasm for fresh air was a hardship stoically endured by those in attendance on her, privately admitted that at 8,000 feet, the Hotel Furca was 'miserably cold and cheerless', while the 'rough and narrow' road to Engelberg over which she made two excursions was 'an unpleasant, tedious *nervous* road'. Her Highland servant, John Brown, who sat at the back of the Sociable on a specially added dicky seat, 'got out and walked near the carriage, whenever we came to particularly steep and precipitous parts'.

Of the many available carriages, the Balmoral Sociable, as it is now called, would have been the ideal one to have taken on such a demanding tour. It is medium-sized, well sprung and seats up to four passengers, with room for a guide or groom on the box beside the coachman. It is easy to manoeuvre and fitted with a strong ratchet brake. There are low doors on both sides and an excellent waterproof hood and apron.

Built by Cook & Holdway of London, the Sociable is the only vehicle painted green in the Royal Collection. It has remained upholstered in the private Balmoral tartan as it was in Queen Victoria's day. Later it was used by her grandson, King George V, to drive to Crathie Church on Sundays during Scottish holidays.

Today there is no sign of John Brown's dicky seat, and extra hooks at the back only indicate the presence of the box Queen Victoria had put on all her sociables to hold picnic baskets. However, a silver plaque inside the vehicle records the highest points reached during a family holiday that must have shown the younger royal children a different world from the secluded gloom that had prevailed at Balmoral, Osborne and Windsor since the Prince Consort's death seven years before.

Opposite The Balmoral tartan is a private one designed by Prince Albert after the purchase of Balmoral Castle in 1852. It is used on the Balmoral estate and worn by members of The Queen's immediate family.

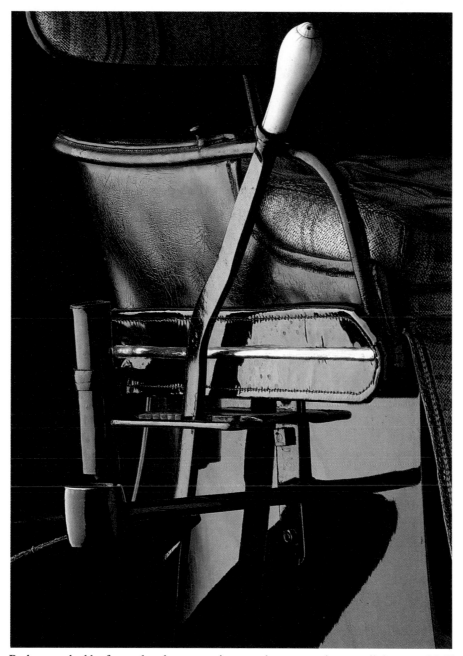

Brakes, worked by foot or hand, were not in general use on carriages until the second half of the nineteenth century. The ratchet lever was a popular design, although the ivory handle on this one is unusual. The brake requires careful application to balance the carriage behind the horses when going downhill.

The first official grant of a coat of arms to Australia was made by King Edward VII in 1908. The shield is quartered with devices representing the six states and surrounded by an ermine border to signify their federation. The supporters, the kangaroo and the emu, identify the arms as being exclusively Australian.

19 The Australian State Coach, 1988

'It is a fitting product of the materials and skills of Australia,
and in our Bicentennial Year portrays the history and craftsmanship
of the best in the light of twentieth-century technology.'

Mr T. A. Slattery, Mayor of Dubbo,
11 February 1988

The first idea that Australia should present Her Majesty with a specially designed state coach as a gift to mark the Bicentenary Year was suggested in March 1986 by a former Mews employee, Australian-born Jim Frecklington. Now working as a coachbuilder in Dubbo, a prosperous country town in New South Wales, Frecklington opened discussions with the Queen's Private Secretary, Sir William Heseltine, and the Australian Government. Before The Queen agreed to accept the vehicle Frecklington had to guarantee that the project was totally funded and that no cost would be incurred by the taxpayers or Government of Australia. With an estimate of over £120,000, Frecklington persuaded the Australia and New Zealand Banking Group to underwrite the cost, which he later recouped through commercial sponsorship and a trust set up by the bank to receive public donations. For $20 or more, contributors' names were recorded in a leather-bound register now on display in the Royal Mews.

Once the finance was secured and Her Majesty's consent obtained, Frecklington gathered together from the state of New South Wales a group of master craftsmen and their associates and started work on the project.

The decision was taken to build a postilion vehicle able to travel and contend with worldwide changes in temperature and humidity. As the first royal state coach to be built since 1902, it was to combine traditional craftsmanship with twentieth-century technology.

With this in mind, measurements were taken from the existing Irish State Coach and 1902 State Landau. To avoid the risk of cracked panels, the body was constructed in steel and aluminium, while the wheels and undercarriage were built on traditional lines from suitable Australian hardwoods. Elm burr veneer was used to border the interior woodwork. Throughout the construction, immense thought was given to the carriage's historical identification with Australia, and indigenous wildflowers were carved and cast in bronze to form the gold-plated roof gallery.

The finished coach was formally presented to The Queen during her tour of the country's Bicentennial celebrations, and the only thing Australia lacked was a suitable team of horses with which to try it out. Delivered to the Mews in August 1988, the coach was put to a postilion-ridden team and, after suitable trials, was first seen by the general public when it was used by Her Majesty to attend the State Opening of Parliament in November 1988.

Her Majesty The Queen travels for the first time in the Australian State Coach to the State Opening of Parliament on 22 November 1988.

The quarter panel is decorated with Her Majesty's Commonwealth insignia. The heraldic work was handpainted by Mr G. C. Francis who travelled to Australia to do this.

LIST OF ITEMS REQUIRED TO BE LOADED FOR THE DRIVING DISPLAY IN COPENHAGEN.

To load on the freight vehicle. Registration. E595AJO

The Australian State Coach complete with lamps, pole, 2 sets of pole pieces.
Batteries to be fitted as arranged by E. West.
Cleaning equipment as necessary as arranged by D. Poole.

Six sides of Black horse state harness.
Two side of Queen's harness as spares.
Three Round Buckle harness bridles and breastplates.
Three posting cruppers.
Eight sides of Ascot harness stowed in four harness boxes.
Three sets of Ascot outrider appointments.
Eight horse collars.
Four saddles.
Eight riding bridles.
One set of lungeing kit.
Six leg irons and postilion whips.
Three outrider whips.

Livery will be covered as follows:
Gmn. Matthews, R. Chambers, M. Chard, D. Oates, A. Myers, D. Pope will take
the livery required to cover anyone's position incase of sickness.
Black Livery for Postilion, Outrider or Horseholder duties. (Kersey breeches)
Postilion Full state jackets, Cap and wig. White breeches. Top boots.
Scarlet Coats. Laced hats, black trousers, ankle boots.

Head Coachman D. Poole, L. Oates to take the following:
Black livery with trousers. Black top hat. Black trousers and ankle boots.
Scarlet, Laced hat, Black trousers and ankle boots.

Eight best day rugs.
Eight blue waterproof rugs.
Eight buckets.
Nine men's personal suit cases.
Brewing up kit.

To be loaded on to the horsebox. Registration. ASO151Y

Eight horses. in travelling gear. Jute rugs to folded and taken.
Eight haynets (Horsehage to be fed)
Eight stable head collars and ropes.
Eight Passports for the horses.
Eight stable logs for stall tying if necessary.
Three buckets.
Grooming kit and mucking out kit. Shampoo.
Eight riding bridles, to walk horses out with.
Veterinary kit - Shoeing kit. Two skips. Six Hunper dumpers.
Hoof oils and brush

The Irish firm of Waterford Crystal were responsible for the hand blown, cut and etched glass on all the lamps. Each exterior carriage lamp carries a slightly different profile of The Queen's head. The brass lamps are copies of ones lent from the Royal Mews.

Since it was built the coach has frequently been displayed at public events.

The Queen's cypher is seen on the roller bolts of the Australian State Coach. Roller bolts are the fittings on the splinter bar to which the harness traces are attached.

Instead of using the traditional methods of carriage painting and varnishing, the vehicle was sprayed with acrylic paint, the heraldic work and gilding pencil-varnished. Colour swatches of royal claret and signal red were sent to Dubbo, so that the correct livery colours could be made up.

Inside the coach, the windows, lighting and thermostatic heating are controlled by a hand panel operated from batteries concealed underneath the footman's seat.

The customary sway of the cee-spring suspension is stabilised by the modern hydraulic system underneath the coach.

185

20 Royal Phantoms

'I hope you will never allow any of those horrible machines
to be used in my stables.'

Queen Victoria to the Duke of Portland,
Master of the Horse (1886–92, 1895–1905)

The first royal motor car ever purchased was bought by King Edward VII in 1901, the year of his accession, although he did not use it in an official capacity.

The bodywork of the early motor cars was little different from that of traditional horsedrawn carriages. They were regarded as the futuristic playthings of the rich, and coachmen and grooms instructed to drive and maintain cars often found themselves quite unsuited to dealing with horse power under the bonnet. The riding and carriage accidents caused by unfamiliarity with these noisy, evil-smelling apparitions made it difficult for people to accept that, from the early twentieth century, the use of the horse and carriage as a method of transport was in gradual decline.

In the Royal Mews, King Edward VII set up the first motor garage, and by 1920 King George V had converted two coachhouses to accommodate the royal Daimlers. The association with Daimler was to last for over forty years. However, since 1950 Rolls Royce have built The Queen's official cars.

The five official Rolls Royce Phantoms live in the back mews. Painted in the livery colours of royal claret and black, the cars carry no registration number plates and are referred to as Rolls Royce Number One, Two, Three, Four or Five. Always garaged in numerical order, each Phantom has a numbered locker which ensures that relevant items are not, in the words of the Head Chauffeur, 'left lying about on a bench'.

Although they are occasionally lent out to other members of the Royal Family, cars One and Two are normally kept for the use of The Queen.

The car most constantly used for official occasions by Her Majesty is Rolls Royce Number One, a 1978 Phantom VI presented to The Queen to commemorate her Silver Jubilee by the Society of Motor Manufacturers and Traders. This is followed by Numbers Two and Three, identical Phantom Vs, built in 1961 and 1960. Similar in shape to the Number One Phantom, either of these cars can be used when necessary as The Queen's car. The other two official Rolls Royces are Number Four, a 1987 Phantom VI and Number Five, a 1950 Phantom IV.

The black hard tops of Rolls Royces One, Two and Three can be unclipped and folded into the boot, leaving a clear perspex roof. Although this can make the car hot in bright sunshine, it gives an excellent all-round view. These cars are also fitted with interior fluorescent lighting and have a raised roofline for ease of movement inside.

Her Majesty is only driven by the Head Chauffeur or the Deputy Head, under whom there are four 'first' chauffeurs, who are required to drive other members of the Royal Family. There are six 'second' chauffeurs for general duties and one of the first things they are taught is how to wash a car properly. Every car is washed (with cold water running through the sponge) and valeted each time it is returned to the garage.

Through the Crown Equerry, the Head Chauffeur co-ordinates the duties of the garage staff with the requirements of Her Majesty's engagements. It is not, however, until the royal cars leave the Mews quadrangle that the twentieth century takes over. Inside the Mews gates even a Rolls Royce Phantom must give way to horses.

Opposite Outside The Queen's private garden entrance at Buckingham Palace. The Number One Rolls Royce waiting for her is a 1978 Phantom VI.

Myth, Kelpie and Spark do *not* go on official occasions.

The Royal Standard can be raised and lowered from inside the driving compartment. It is flown at all times when Her Majesty is in the car, except when travelling on motorways. The car is never driven with the shield uncovered and standard raised if Her Majesty is not present.

188

The Queen's personal silver mascot of St George and the dragon was especially designed for her by the artist Edward Seago. It is mounted on whichever of the Phantoms Her Majesty is using at the time. When consecutive methods of transport are being used, the mascot is carried off the train, yacht or plane ahead of The Queen and screwed onto the Rolls Royce waiting to continue the engagement.

21 Christmas

London and South East:
Cloudy with rain, heavy at times, drier later.
Winds south west moderate to strong.

The *Daily Telegraph* Weather Report,
14th December

The photographs for this book have been taken between January and December. The final shoot is tonight, when the Mews holds its annual Christmas party for friends, staff and families, complete with hot soup and chestnuts. The private gathering, informally attended by Her Majesty whenever possible, takes place in the quadrangle, and here the evening's highlight is the arrival of Father Christmas in a horse-drawn sleigh, piped into the yard by The Queen's Piper. A frame of this scene has been in our mind's eye for the last year to provide the perfect ending to the book.

The Victorian pair-horse sleigh made by Bruno Ledoux & Co of Montreal has spent the last week with the carriage restorers. Because of *the photograph* this year's decoration is the result of much combined concentration and effort. Now, covered in glue and glitter, it lies hidden in the back mews.

Inside the Paint Shop, our project base for the past twelve months, David Cripps and his assistant mutter, deep in their box of tricks. Cushioned by tea and cigarettes, they try to ignore the wind and the drizzle outside.

George IV's quadrangle and William IV's gas lights are hung with strings of coloured lights. On the Gold State Coach, George III's tritons blow their fanfare, anticipating the appearance of Father Christmas on the dais beside the traditionally decorated Christmas tree, something that Prince Albert introduced into this country.

In the State Stable, final adjustments are being made to the harness and mane dressings of the horses who will draw the sleigh. Peter, whose temperament makes him a constant choice for the daily Messenger Brougham, did the same job last year. Now aged fifteen, he looks resigned as bells and tinsel are attached to his harness. Next to him, Twilight's ten-year-old knees show no sign of his summer mishap; he slipped and was pulled down in the wheel of the 1902 as it turned into Victoria Street during a state visit.

Around the back mews, Father Christmas – a professional for the past forty years – exercises his white samoyed. He volunteers the information that this is his twentieth Mews Christmas. Dressed as 'Snow Queen' and 'dog handler', his seven-year-old twin grandchildren help to hoist the sack of presents into the sleigh.

Meanwhile the quadrangle fills with groups who wander in and out of harness rooms and stables asking questions. Resplendent in best rugs and headcollars, the pillar-reined bay horses are much admired. Opposite them, Civil Service horses munch hay in darkness. Liveried helpers in drab coats and top hats mingle around the coal braziers in the quadrangle, helping with the pushchairs, babies and children.

In the loose boxes, some horses are celebrating their first royal Christmas. Barbados, a three-year-old Gelderlander, is wary of swinging lanterns and carols sung in English. The grey Alderney is, however, more relaxed; aged six, his calm expression befits the postilion-ridden leader of the all-Dutch team put to the Queen of the Netherlands' carriage on her summer visit.

Opposite Horse-drawn sleighs were introduced into the Mews by Prince Albert. There are still six in the Royal Collection.

The rain has stopped and, having warmed up their voices in the main coachhouse, Lady Aldington's choir invite us to 'Hark!' with the herald angels in the quadrangle stables. Charmed by mangers and music, it goes unnoticed that outside the photographers are coping with polythene sheeting, wind and more rain. We only discover this when we come out into the quadrangle again. The tannoy urges the children to shout for Father Christmas and the first notes of the Piper are heard. The sky clears, a final lighting test is made, eyes are glued to cameras and we wait.

Then, suddenly, a blinding flash . . . the unusual sight of David Cripps running turns optimism to horror. 'There's a fuse blown – stop the sleigh!' But the children's blood is up; they have waited long enough. From under Nash's Doric arch the perfect picture comes. As instructed, the procession slowly passes the book team at an angle guaranteed for photographic success. Without the lighting, the pre-set cameras are useless; water in a wet extension socket has blown the fuse – and a priceless picture.

Questions are being asked on all sides; the staff of the Mews who have laughed with us, at us and for us are as doleful as we are. Fuses can be mended, but Father Christmas, now immersed in present-giving, is no longer available.

Having received their gifts, the children pack into the sleigh for rides around the quadrangle. We realise that this is our last chance to capture the vehicle and any remaining atmosphere on film. The best background is the chosen one, coming through the arch. Persuaded to do so again, the horses, unsettled by the tricky manoeuvre of turning the sledge on its fixed iron wheels, speed unevenly past our lights. The tripods swing: 'Only three frames.' There just might be one we can use.

The party eventually ends and, crossing the empty quadrangle as the coloured lights are turned off, resignation sets in. Ah, well . . . Father Christmas? He always was an elusive character.